Self-Discipline, Jealousy and Anger Management

(Three Book Box Set)

Ryan James

Additionally, the information in the following pages is intended only for informational purposes and should thus be thought of as universal. As befitting its nature, it is presented without assurance regarding its prolonged validity or interim quality. Trademarks that are mentioned are done without written consent and can in no way be considered an endorsement from the trademark holder.

Table of Contents
Self-Discipline

Jealousy

Anger Management

Self-Discipline

*32 Small Changes to Create a Life Long Habit
Of Self-Discipline,
Laser-Sharp Focus, And Extreme Productivity*

Introduction

Here's one surprising fact about self-discipline: people who have it are generally happier than those who don't.

It's true. You'd think that not allowing yourself to give in to every impulse, every hedonistic urge and just doing everything you like and saying everything you want to say will make you one happy camper. But no, a <u>2013 study</u> showed the complete opposite.

People with high self-control are in fact more content with their lives. They are well-adjusted, sociable, and are more likely to make excellent decisions. They make great leaders. They live a harmonious life with their partners. This is not to say that they don't feel miserable. They experience unhappiness. They face disappointments. They deal with conflict. However, self-disciplined people do not allow these emotions to get in the way of what they want in life. They have laser sharp focus and they always have their eyes on the prize – and more often than not, they get it!

It seems like they have life figured out even though they probably don't think about it that way.

The whole notion of self-discipline might be off-putting. It just seems like something that is too difficult to achieve.

But the truth is, anyone can develop self-discipline and take back his life.

But you should not view it as one insurmountable mountain. Instead, take one step at a time. This is exactly why we created this guide on the 32 small changes you can make in order to achieve self-discipline.

You can learn, develop, and improve self-discipline through daily practice and a regimen of good habits. You can live free and break your bad habits through repetitive simple changes to your daily routine in all areas of your life. You don't have to make drastic changes. You can start with small things and soon you will have the confidence to apply discipline in all areas of your life.

You may have chosen this book because you have finally decided to take control of your life – and what better place to start than with yourself? Perhaps, you chose to read this book because you don't want to feel helpless anymore. Whatever your reasons may be, it is never too late to start practicing self-discipline.

Your Free Gift

As a way of saying thanks for your purchase, I wanted to offer you a free bonus E-book called *"How to Talk to Anyone: 50 Best Tips and Tricks to Build Instant Rapport"*.

Within this comprehensive guide, you will find information on:

- How to make a killer first impression
- Tips on becoming a great listener
- Using the FORM method for asking good questions
- Developing a great body language
- How to never run out of things to say
- Bonus chapters on Persuasion, Emotional Intelligence, and How to Analyze People

To grab your free bonus book just <u>tap here</u>, or go to:

<u>http://ryanjames.successpublishing.club/freebonus/</u>

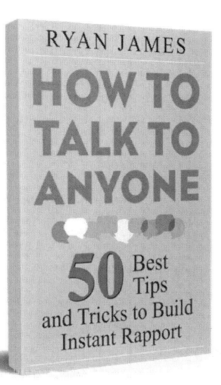

Part 1:

A Closer Look at Self-Discipline

Contrary to popular belief, self-discipline is not about limiting yourself. It's about having the capability to act according to what you know you should (which is in line with your goals in life) instead of letting your feelings dictate your actions. It is about self-mastery.

When the average person thinks of self-discipline, he usually conjures up images of a scary drill sergeant giving you hell for not polishing your boots enough or not standing straight enough. That's not self-discipline.

The One Thing You Need To Know Before Getting Started

But self-discipline is not just about complying with "rules". It is a lifetime commitment to staying in line with what you want in life. It entails fighting that desire for instant gratification. It entails maintaining your motivation. It's about being in there for the long haul.

The key word here is commitment.

You need to know that it's not something you suddenly get and then you're set for life.

But don't worry though because self-discipline *can* be learned.

Self-discipline is not innate. Think about it: a toddler does not have self-control. When he wants to do or get something, he is motivated to do it or go after it. A small child initially has no regard for the consequences of his actions. But as he grows older and is trained by his parents, influenced by his environment, starts to desire the positive reactions from the people around him, he will learn about cause and effect, restrictions, rules, and authority. Hopefully, he will learn to apply self-discipline to his choices and actions.

You can learn self-discipline – anyone can. The change we will mention in this book is just to get you started. The things we will talk about in this book do not require you to buy or prepare anything – you only need to be ready to commit.

In the following chapters, you will learn just "how" to do that by making small changes in your daily life.

Debunking Myths About Self-Discipline

Before going into detail about how we can improve our sense of self-discipline through practical tips and exercises, we must first try to debunk the common myths and misconceptions that are associated with it. Otherwise, our false understanding might prevent us from learning further.

There are so many wrong notions about self-discipline. For example, we regard it as the need to live a strict and controlled lifestyle – a rigid, difficult, and demanding process. But, these thoughts don't help at all in making us appreciate the value of this virtue, and might even cause us to give up what we have not even started.

If you haven't been well-disciplined in the past then, yes, you might find following through somewhat hard – at first. But, it is not unlikely because self-discipline is not supposed to make things any more difficult for us. It's us who are making it more difficult for ourselves by doing the opposite!

Yet another misconception that we have about self-discipline is of it being inherent to a person, and that unless you have it then you are probably better without it. But, such a belief could only make us passive about the idea of being disciplined and strong-willed. This is even worse.

Are you ready to throw some light on the subject of self-discipline? The common myths and false beliefs that people associate with it as a trait and as a habit are listed below. When viewed from a fresh perspective, however, self-discipline can change your life.

Myth #1: Discipline forms good habits then it becomes a habit

One misconception that many people have about self-discipline is that it is similar to habit-forming. We tend to think that by sticking to a certain habit then we are already practicing self-discipline.

This is not usually the case, however.

Sticking to a certain diet plan or workout is a habit, but so is having your lunch or dinner at a specific time every day. Studying daily even when it is not examination week is a habit, but so is waking up at the same time every day to go to school.

So, basically, almost everything that we do routinely is a habit, but they don't always equate to having self-discipline!

What exactly is self-discipline, then?

The Truth: Discipline is what forms good habits and vice versa

Only by debunking these myths about self-discipline will we truly understand what it means to have it deep-seated in our characters, and one such misconception is about it being equivalent to the term "habit".

As was illustrated above, things that we habitually do are simply habits and practicing them unfailingly does not make us disciplined individuals. Instead, it is the other way around.

A good example of this is dieting – starting a regimen and sticking by it until you've achieved your desired results (weight loss, leaner physique).

With dieting, you will be forming certain habits along the way. It won't be that easy, though, without self-discipline.

Self-discipline is what would make you commit to the diet plan, whatever the diet is. Be it a low-carb/high-protein, purely vegan, or raw food diet, won't really matter. What matters is that you adhere to the plan until you've reached your goal (e.g. 3% weight loss after a month) or way beyond that.

Also at this point, you've most likely already established good habits and following through them is no longer big deal. Only goes to show that habits are actually just actions formed. Self-discipline, however, is the mind-set that allows us to form these habits and commit to them.

Myth #2: Some people are born with "it", some aren't

Some people regard self-discipline as something that is totally out of our hand -- you either have it or that you don't.

In line with this, we also tend to think that only some people have and are capable of self-discipline, and that it is something only a lucky few have been born with. We think of self-discipline as something that is too hard to achieve and then just succumb to the belief that it may be not for us.

This mind-set then becomes a catalyst for life-long problems. When we start to accept that self-discipline is an elusive virtue inherent only to some, we are subconsciously depriving ourselves of chances to succeed because we don't actively challenge ourselves to become better.

Without self-discipline, we will just do what we want, say what we want, or eat what we want with little or no regard of whether we are doing the right thing or not. We don't actively avoid temptations. We lose control in some areas of life (e.g. health, career), but we believe otherwise and are blind.

Without an actual sense of control over ourselves, or at least the belief that we can achieve it, we are "just humans" and not persons thus success becomes much more elusive to us than self-discipline ever has been.

The Truth: Self-discipline is not inborn – it can be developed

As a well-known philosopher once said, "The first and best victory is to conquer self." This is the main principle behind self-discipline.

Plato's famous quote may not exactly and solely be referring to self-discipline, but he captured the essence of it nonetheless.

In reality, self-discipline is not inherent. It is something that we can learn, attain, develop, and even gain mastery of no matter who we are or where we are in life.

Self-discipline is having the ability to conquer ourselves by allowing ourselves to be bound by certain rules, whether we like these rules or not, so long as they result in positive outcomes. An example of this is going to the gym regularly to stay fit even if you find it hard and dislike it a little.

Applying self-discipline in everyday life can be difficult but not impossible. It is a conscious effort, not a dream. Any person can certainly become self-disciplined.

Myth #3: Certain Life Conditions Affect Self-Discipline

Sometimes, it is the belief that self-discipline is bound by certain conditions or life situations that prevents us from actively pursuing it.

Say for example, we believe that the older we get, the more self-disciplined we are bound to become. Or, well-educated people are more likely to learn self-discipline easier than those who did not finish school.

Even on the subject of self-discipline, we tend to be somewhat discriminatory.

The Truth: The struggle to achieve self-discipline is universal

A recent study by Southwestern Consulting, in partnership with Kelton Global Research, revealed that there is no specific demographic trait that makes a person more or less likely to succeed in changing habits.

Specifically, age, gender, marital status, education level, and geographic location all have no significant bearing on predicting a person's success rate in achieving self-discipline. Simply put, "struggling with self-discipline is universal."

While this is something good to know, the same research group also found out that those who kept the resolution for at least 30 days are more likely to follow through for a year – or more!

Therefore, it is not your current life condition that would determine if you are to become self-disciplined or not. Young and old, rich and poor – everyone has an equal chance for any change. It is just a matter of proper mindset and being able to condition yourself for the positive changes that you are about to create.

Now that we have a better understanding of what self-discipline is all about, the next phases of this book will focus more on its practice – how we can apply it to our daily lives, how it is associated with our common experiences and more importantly, how we can create a life-long habit of it.

Part 2:

The 32 Changes Small Changes That Will Take You Places

Developing new habits can be difficult and making a permanent change may sometimes seem impossible. But, there is a reason why some people fail with habit development – and it is not the lack of self-discipline.

It is, as a matter of fact, our frantic attempt to change multiple habits at the same time. We tend to apply what we learn about self-help and building good habits by trying to change our old ways all at once.

While there is nothing wrong with wanting to improve, focusing on multiple habits requires a lot of mental strength which some of us may not be capable of sustaining, resulting in mental and emotional exhaustion.

What, therefore, is the best solution?

The best way to develop life-long habits is by starting with small, manageable changes and just building upon them as you go along.

This doesn't mean that these steps are easy. It just means that there is no need for drastic changes. You only need to consider making these small doable changes that anyone can certainly accomplish.

Remember that the keyword here is *life-long*. Short spurts of situational willpower will get us nowhere!

Yes, we can stay motivated for a certain amount of time or when we need it the most, but without forming long term self-discipline habits we are simply to go round in circles – it'll be like being back to square one all the time.

There is a saying that goes, "Life is a marathon, not a sprint." Likewise, our self-discipline goals should be focused on developing life-long self-discipline within us, and it is possible! Slowly but surely we can, and there are 32 small changes that we can start with today to guarantee just that.

Shaping Your Mind for Self-Discipline

Conditioning yourself for discipline is quite important. You have to be prepared for it and, of course, you have to have the desire for it. Otherwise, it won't become a habit.

Additionally, acquiring the right mentality is just as vital as doing actual exercises because without it, you just might not be able to follow through.

So, having the right attitude to start with is a key ingredient for succeeding in this endeavor. The following sections comprise the first small changes that will prepare you for building a life-long habit of self-discipline.

1. Don't wait for the right moment.

This is the first stumbling block for many people who are trying to build self-discipline. The thing is, right at the very beginning, you will feel stirrings of discomfort. It is human nature to be resistant to change. Even your brain will not want you to suddenly do something different from what it has been so used to doing. Behaviors related to habits are usually processed in the basal ganglia – it's that part of your brain that handles patterns and memories.

Decision making, however, is processed by the prefrontal cortex which is a completely different area. So you see, even at a biological level, your habits and your decisions are already at odds. If you're already used to doing something, you could just operate on auto-pilot. The decision to change a routine, however, requires you to be on another level – it requires you to be completely mentally present. It requires focus *and* resolve.

So what should you do? First, you should expect that you will be talking yourself into abandoning the plan – be that to be more disciplined, or to commit to a diet, or to go to the gym that day. Be prepared for that moment by talking back to those little voices -- they're just your basal ganglia talking.

Remember: the right moment does not exist. You should not wait for it.

What you need to do is to start anyway. Don't obsess about finishing.

If it's incredibly hard, trick yourself by saying things that would make it easier. For example, if you planned to go to the gym but you kept putting it off, worrying about what the ripped guys would say or how awful you'd look on the treadmill.

Tell yourself that you only need to go to the gym – you don't have to work out. You can just sit there, but you absolutely have to go to the gym. Don't think about what you'll be doing there. Just focus on getting to the gym. By doing that step, you will be actively making a decision and forcing yourself out of auto-pilot.

You can develop self-discipline by changing what you do on a daily basis – and you need to start somewhere. When you make an active decision and follow through it in the simple things, you will acquire the right behavior and build a new habit.

2. Start small a.k.a. use the 1-minute rule

This one is a little like tricking yourself into starting, but in a different way. However, it's also about jarring yourself out of auto pilot and forcing your mind to do active thinking.

Sometimes, it is hard to do the things you know you have to do such as working out or doing chores. Some projects are downright intimidating while some tasks are just so unappealing you – or no one else on the planet – don't really want to do them.

But you know you have to. So what can you do to get started? Resolve to do just one teeny part of it – something that usually takes just ONE minute.

If there's a huge pile of dirty dishes, tell yourself you'll only be cleaning 1 or 2 – just enough to have something to use for dinner. Say, you have to declutter. Just tell yourself that you only need to throw away 3 things and that's it.

You'll find it easier to start that way. It may seem like you're doing such a small thing but you'll soon discover that you're actually building motivation and confidence to continue. Eventually, you'll notice that doing that task is something that actually makes you feel good (yes, even mundane tasks like doing the dishes can give a sense of accomplishment) and that will help build self-discipline.

Remember that you need to develop self-discipline by doing something on a regular basis. You can try this trick to give yourself that extra push to do something.

3. Accept that there is a need to change

To change your behavior, you need to be aware that you are in need of such change. It may sound simple but in reality, many people usually struggle with this too.

Denying it to ourselves that something has to change or simply not realizing the need for it may mean that we're happy and content with the *status quo*. After all, what change are we after when there is nothing wrong or lacking?

Say, you're thinking about whether you really need to start dieting. The need for some diet modification usually starts with being aware that you are already becoming overweight, or that you no longer fit into most of your jeans.

Without realizing or acknowledging what needs to be changed, however, then we probably aren't after any goal. On the other hand, being aware of what must be done may actually prompt us to take action (e.g., changing diets, starting a fitness plan).

You can lie all you want to other people, but try not to lie to yourself.

You can force yourself to face this by collecting concrete information. Get on the weight scale. Calculate how many calories you tend to take on a daily basis. Take pictures and acknowledge that it's not the unflattering angle that is the problem.

Acknowledge your weaknesses. Nobody's perfect. You've heard that so many times but that doesn't make it any less true.

Whether you know that you can't resist a good burger, or that you're an alcoholic, you need to acknowledge your pitfalls. Do not try to minimize their impact on your life.

Self-discipline starts with acknowledging the need for change, is carried out through this change, and is achieved when we've started to form positive habits and behaviors.

4. Set Clear Goals

You didn't just wake up today with resolve to have self-discipline and ended up reading this book. You're here because you want to have self-discipline. There's no question on that. But here's one question you need to answer:

What exactly do you need to accomplish so badly that you have resolved to build self-discipline?

You need to provide a clear answer to that question so that you can formulate the right strategy.

Goals have to be SMART – specific, measurable, attainable, results-focused, and more importantly, time bound. So if your goal is to exercise more often, that won't do. Don't get me wrong; that's good enough as a starting point but that's not enough if you want to commit.

This is an example of a smart goal related to exercising:

1. I want to lose 40 pounds in one year so I can finally look in the mirror without hating myself.

It is specific and measurable (40 pounds lost which you can track through). It is attainable (after all, you can safely lose weight if it's 1 pound a week). It's results-focused (weight loss to look good and have self-esteem) and the time frame is one year.

You can create a plan based on that long-term goal.

You could create short-term goals that would serve as stepping stones. For example, your short term goals would be:

1. To cut on soda consumption on the first week

2. To lose 1 pound on the first month

When you set these goals, make a plan of action and stick to it as you undertake a task.

5. Know what drives you.

There are two kinds of motivation – intrinsic and extrinsic. Intrinsic motivation is brought by your own will and desire to perform a given activity. Extrinsic motivation is brought by external punishments or rewards. You need to know this because of one important reason:

Extrinsic motivation is likely to corrode self-discipline while intrinsic motivation can help strengthen it.

To illustrate, say, your job entails pitching a marketing plan to clients. A person whose motivation is to "create a marketing plan that will blow the client's mind" has intrinsic motivation. For that person, the reward is the act of developing something great. A person whose motivation is to "create a marketing plan so I don't get fired" isn't likely to be able to maintain a desire to perform well. He would deliver, sure, but to the detriment of his emotional health.

Intrinsic motivation builds self-discipline because it doesn't make you feel deprived. Instead, it makes you feel in control because it makes you feel engaged, excited, and on control of the direction your life is heading. It gives you confidence and makes you more creative. It boosts your self-esteem and overall well-being.

Note that this isn't always black and white. Some tasks are inherently unpleasant that a person can summon very little intrinsic motivation.

Now, what if the only reward you can see is extrinsic? In that case, you need to shape your mind in order to internalize those external motivations.

For example, you absolutely hate brainstorming for marketing plans but you know you have to. However, if you come to understand how doing that task can add value to you – as a person – instead of it merely being a paycheck – then it can be internalized. Whenever you have to do that task and you find yourself hating it, think about how it is slowly making you more valuable in your workplace and how it's helping you grow your skills. Make it about you – not just something you have to do.

So to build discipline, think about the *whys* and *hows*. Why do you do things and how could those things help you get to your long term goals?

6. Learn how to deal with temptations

Temptations abound. There is always the desire to do or have something you know you shouldn't. It is a constant in life but it is something that even well-disciplined individuals need to overcome. The ability to resist it equates to having good self-discipline.

Resisting temptations, however, is easier said than done. You can see it everywhere - many people fall out of their diet plans because they couldn't resist going back to their old eating habits. A lot of relationships end due to cheating because it's easier to give in to temptation than to fight it.

The good news is that while temptations are everywhere around us, dealing with them effectively is something that we can learn, and there are many ways to do so.

Evaluating your motivations is also important in dealing with temptations. Say you started a diet plan with the end goal of losing weight, but boxes of chocolates recently arrived just for you. Is your motivation to reach your end goal stronger than your desire to eat chocolates?

If you happened to choose the latter then it means that your end goal is not enticing enough – you need a stronger source of motivation. How about being more specific with your objective?

Instead of simply saying that "to lose weight" is your goal, set a specific value for that weight (e.g. 120 lbs. or lower in 2 months), and have a mental picture of how you would like to see yourself in a month. Will you achieve your desired physique if you give in to what's tempting you now?

There is a problem with motivation though – sometimes, it isn't enough. Sometimes, you need more than a powerful reason to stick to your goals and fight temptations.

Go out of your way to avoid temptation

The most effective technique, however, is actually staying away from the source of temptation whenever possible, or simply removing temptation you cannot stay away from.

Avoiding temptation requires anticipating situations where unwanted desires might emerge and taking proactive steps to ensure that one doesn't succumb to the problematic desire.

For example, avoiding exposure to tempting situations can include making unhealthy foods less visible, such as keeping one's home free of unhealthy but tempting foods.

Why come down to choosing between eating chocolates and sticking to your pre-summer diet plan when you can just clean up your pantry and get rid of all unhealthy food. Stop buying chocolates when you know that you could be tempted to eat them.

Actions that you can try:

- ❖ Stay as far from the source of temptation as possible (e.g. away from the kitchen/fridge when you are always tempted to eat or from the mall when you are about to be broke)
- ❖ Keep your temptations buried – or frozen (e.g. leaving your credit card at home buried under piles of laundry or, better yet, just freezing it – literally or figuratively – it's all up to you)
- ❖ Destroy your temptation! (e.g. cutting that credit half onto half and resolving to use cash or debit card moving forward)

The truth is, it might take some time before you fully learn how to resist your greatest temptations, especially the temptation to overindulge in things (food, shopping, unhealthy lifestyle, etc.), but if you build inner strength and self-discipline, you will eventually learn to overcome them.

7. **Manage Stress to reinforce self-control**

While staying motivated is helpful in resisting temptations, you can't always rely on it, especially if you're motivated by extrinsic motivation. Stress management can help you regain a feeling of control.

Studies show that stress can make us extremely poor at self-control, thereby making us less resistant to temptations and more accepting of gratifying actions, even if these meant developing bad behaviors and losing our overall sense of self-discipline.

A good example of this is binge-eating or getting drunk due to stress (in the office or at home) wherein the affected person deals with his negative feelings by consuming more food than usual or by taking in alcohol. This otherwise disciplined individual succumbed to such actions in response to the stressful situation.

While some people are good at managing stress and even perform better under stressful conditions, some simply cannot handle it. But, it is good to know that there are many ways through which we can reduce the stress in our lives – without losing control and sacrificing our sense of self-discipline. These include:

- ❖ Going for a walk (walking somehow helps clear the mind, especially nature walks)
- ❖ Meditating (the power of meditation to be discussed later)
- ❖ Getting a massage or some pampering (e.g. haircut, manicure)

- ❖ Spending time with family and friends, and getting a good laugh
- ❖ Reading books and watching feel-good movies

Find a way to release some tension so you can regain a feeling of self-control. Take one step at a time if you need to and discover other ways to effectively deal with temptation so that you can stay committed to being self-disciplined.

8. Identify your distractions

"He who chases two rabbits catches none" – Confucius

Self-discipline is defined as our ability to take control over our desires and impulses to stay focused on our objectives. Losing focus, on the other hand, compromises the fulfillment of these goals. When we get distracted, we could fail to do what needs to get done, and we lose our sense of self-discipline.

Having that laser-sharp focus is, therefore, one of qualities that we need to develop in order to stay disciplined enough to reach our goals.

Identifying what makes us lose focus (distractions) is only the first step, but is sometimes the hardest to figure out. Let's say you are trying to concentrate on writing a book but finding it hard to do so as you are constantly stopping in the middle of your thoughts. What is it that often triggers you to stop?

Are you simply at a loss for words? Experiencing mental block? Or is it that phone of yours constantly ringing? Or maybe you have Facebook open on another tab and you are constantly tempted to check what that notification is about? Or maybe it is a combination of these things?

By finding out exactly what is distracting you, you can stay on track by consciously removing the things that tend to disrupt your concentration.

Is it your phone? Then put it on silent mode or, better yet, politely inform the other party that you are trying to concentrate on a project. Or is it your Facebook account opened on another tab? Then, by all means, log out and try stay away from all social media channels for a while.

Remember that distractions are obstacles that you need to learn to overcome in order to successfully reach your goals. Otherwise all you'll be left with are just wasted valuable time and energy – exhaustion, delays, failure, sadness, and more problems than you can think of.

Concentration is the opposite of distraction. It is the sustained effort to remain focused.

Once we've identified and removed what has been distracting us, the next step is to concentrate on what needs to get done for us to succeed. To help improve or maintain this concentration, however, there are other things that we can do, including:

- ❖ Decluttering to remove distractions
- ❖ Destressing to help clear the mind
- ❖ Snapping back quickly into whatever you're doing as your mind starts to wander

The following section features an exercise that you can do in order to be mindful of distractions.

9. Use the timer technique to kill urges with mindfulness

Every once in a while, you'll experience the urge to just quit doing something you don't like or to temporarily stop and just go watch cat videos on YouTube. Cat videos are fun and all but those urges would only harm your efforts to build self-discipline.

What you can do is to develop mindfulness so that you can quickly catch yourself when there is an impulse to do something else and give up on a task you should be working on.

You can do this by setting a specific time where you acknowledge that the only thing you should be working on is a certain task, say a quarterly report, or a chapter on the novel you're writing. Say, you are allocating 10 minutes of mindfulness while doing that task. Pay attention to your feelings and observe if the urge to resort to distractions like YouTube or gaming arises.

You'll know when the urge arises because you'll temporarily stop creating content for your report or novel as your mind wanders to the distraction.

However, instead of shaking it off, recognize that the urge did exist but that you're not letting yourself give in to it because the entire span of 10 minutes is dedicated to nothing else but the task you specified.

This is what Raymond Chandler, an American writer, used in order to stay productive. He said he has two rules while the task timer is on: A. He doesn't have to write B. But he can't do anything else.

It works because you're dedicating a specific time period of a task, allowing you to notice when the urges occur because when they do, then there is only one task that is affected – the one you are supposed to be working on and nothing else.

Practice this often in order to develop mindfulness and manage your impulses better.

Building Your Character With These Self-Discipline Habits

Self-discipline takes a lot of inner strength, which is why it is one of the hallmarks of good character.

Having said that, it is also important to stress that character isn't always inborn. Certain characteristics can be learned and character can still be developed.

Moreover, strength of character doesn't develop overnight, nor is it simply acquired when things are easy-going. Character building only becomes more effective in the presence of discomfort, and the only time we are truly growing is when we are exposed to adversity.

10. Exercise Restraint

There is one thing that all people with excellent self-discipline also have – incredible restraint. They know when to stop.

Martin Luther King JR and Mahatma Gandhi, for example, showed restraint while on a quest to bring their people together to take a stand against something – racism in the case of the former and British rule in the latter. Even war heroes such as Dick Winters are known for exercising leadership restraint – they know when to rally their troops and when it's time to give their people – and even enemies -- a reprieve.

Restraint is what allows you to not give in to the things you can easily get. It allows you to make the right decisions and achieve your goals. People who have self-restraint are known to be strong in all the senses of the word.

You can build your restraint by establishing a pattern of behavior. If you're used to lashing out whenever you're having problems at work, accept that you have a problem with your temper and then start actively exhibiting different behavior. When faced with an annoying colleague, before you say or do something hurtful, count from 1 to 10.

Do this multiple times until you create a pattern. Not saying something hurtful that one time will make it easier for you to not say something hurtful the next time.

Surprisingly, having a sugary drink like lemonade can also help. Studies show that your self-control becomes hampered when you have low blood sugar levels. So if you find yourself getting low on willpower and being especially cranky, drink lemonade or munch on an apple.

11. Chase Discomfort

Practicing self-discipline is already a challenge in itself – what more in the presence of difficulties or further challenges?

Say, you've already started a routine and are consistently getting positive outcomes. You've been working out for 8 days.

What happens, though, when you are suddenly faced with a difficult situation? What if you suddenly have to spend several hours at work to manage a crisis and can't be at the gym at the usual hour. Will your habits change?

Many people give up on their diet regimen after realizing all the trouble that they'd have to go through to achieve their ideal body weight. Starting a strictly vegan diet, for example, means that you'll have to plan your meals in advance, prepare differently for trips to the groceries store, research recipes, and call restaurants to find out if they have a vegan menu. All of these things can be challenging especially if you're busy and you're used to the taste of meat.

As mentioned, humans naturally want familiar things, which is why when faced with discomfort, they usually resort to escapism such as TV and video games.

What you can do is to resolve to thrive in discomfort. Actively find ways to be uncomfortable. Relish in the thought that you will be sore after an hour of working out. Try a cold shower for once. Go someplace you've never been to. Find a new bar to hang out it.

You'll see that discomfort does not mean the end of the world.

The more that you acknowledge and accept the difficult situation that you are in, the more likely that you will come to terms with it and take the necessary action.

By allowing yourself to embrace adversity, you are also teaching yourself mental toughness – the ability to mentally withstand difficult situations and to get past them.

12. Rejection Therapy

Rejection is considered as rather negative – both in connotation and the actual feeling. Oftentimes, it is hard to deal with this emotion.

In reality, rejection will always be a part of our lives. At one point, we are going to be turned down, left out, or denied something. This does not only apply to our careers, though, but also to our most important relationships.

What good does rejection do, then?

While it generally hurts, being rejected allows us to grow in character by making us realize that life is not always a bed of roses. It just motivates us to do better, teaches us how to persevere, and keeps us on our toes after a failed interview, an unsuccessful venture, or a bad breakup.

After all, if those situations did not kill us, then we are only going to get stronger, right?

As for the exercise, we can make use of a card game called "Rejection Therapy" (by Jason Comely) which capitalizes on the feelings of rejection. In this game, the only rule is to get rejected at least once every single day.

The cards contain various challenges such as asking women out on dates, requesting for discounts on purchases, asking favors from complete strangers, etc. You are not a winner, though, until you are given a "No".

"Rejection Therapy" is not trying to make rejection sound as if it is a totally delightful experience, nor is it trying to make some fun out of it. Rather, it was designed to allow us to feel rejection until we become desensitized to it.

In general, learning to overcome the discomforts of rejection is already a growth in itself – both in mindset and in character. Moreover, being able to deal with this type of discomfort helps improve our sense of self-discipline through empowerment. The more rejection that we can handle, the more empowered that we become and the more disciplined that we tend to be.

In the chapter on failure, there are a couple of exercises that would allow you to get exposed to the discomforts of rejection.

13. Build Cold Tolerance

Studies show how cold-conditioning could radically improve your health.

In fact, one man from Netherlands, Win Hof, has been using this method to strengthen his mind and body. Now, he is world-renowned for his several ice endeavors and has been given the nickname "The Iceman" for his ability to withstand extremely cold temperatures. His practices include meditation, exposure to cold (often ice cold), and breathing techniques.

Why does he do it, though? Is this man crazy to be working out in the snow?

While building cold tolerance has numerous physical benefits such as strengthened immune system and improved cardiovascular health, it can do wonders for your mind as well. Just like exercise, short term exposure to intense cold conditions creates stress on your body and mind and are, therefore, useful in the practice of self-discipline.

It is not that self-discipline should be stressful, however. The whole point of placing the mind and body under such stress or discomfort is to develop certain behaviors that we can never achieve when life is full of comfort. Hence, cold conditioning is one such exercise that is useful in character building.

The good news is that we don't need to submerge ourselves in ice just to be able to develop forbearance to cold and general physical and mental tolerance. What we can do instead is to try these three exercises as they are equally as effective and great if you are just learning about this technique:

❖ Cold Feet – This involves walking barefoot on cold surfaces. Be careful when walking on snow, though, as you might just get injured from frostbite. Otherwise, going barefoot on chilling grounds is one of the most powerful ways to develop cold tolerance. You can start with three to five minutes of walk a few times each day and keep doing this for a week. You'll then notice that by the end of first week, you have already become accustomed to having cold feet (literally and figuratively) or developed overall tolerance to cold.

❖ Cold Showers – This is yet another exercise involving exposure to cold – a good alternative to the first exercise when the weather outside isn't that chilly. As the name implies, you are supposed to take cold showers. But, it should be regular (daily), timed (5 minutes and up) showers and not when you only feel like doing so. This would require a lot of self-discipline on your part, although it is the simplest way to learn how to handle discomfort.

❖ Cold Walks – This is perhaps the most effective of all three cold exercises and requires walking dressed down (tank top, shorts, sandals or, better yet, barefoot) in a temperature that is rather cold for you or that really pushes you to your limits. Just like cold shower, this must be done regularly for you to develop intense cold acclimation.

This cold conditioning practice is not meant to make the road to self-discipline harder than it should be. Remember that our goal here is to build certain traits that you wouldn't otherwise develop when you are always feeling cozy and comfortable.

Resiliency, better tolerance to physical discomfort, improved mental concentration, greater adaptation to stress – these are just some of the characteristics needed to enhance our self-discipline and that can be developed by exposing ourselves to less favorable conditions.

41

14. **Doing Without Your Usual "Needs"**

All of us have different needs and some of these we simply cannot do without.

A stable job, food on the table and a house to call home – these are just some of the things that we need in order to survive. These are basic necessities.

According to Sir Abraham Maslow, our needs are divided as follows:

- ❖ Physiological (e.g. food, water, rest, shelter)
- ❖ Safety and Security (e.g. health, employment, safety net)
- ❖ Love and Belongingness (e.g. family, friends, intimacy, sense of connection)
- ❖ Self-Esteem (e.g. achievement, promotion, self-confidence)
- ❖ Self-Actualization (e.g. morality, sense of purpose)

The first two needs are both basic and are vital to our existence. The third one, sense of love and belongingness, is also significant to some extent.

How about our other needs, then?

As humans, we tend to exaggerate things. "Dying" of laughter, stress "killing" us, "not surviving" without our phones – you've probably heard these lines before. In reality, though, we could live just fine without the things that we typically exaggerate about needing.

Back to *Maslow's Hierarchy of Needs*, other than the basics, the rest are considered psychological needs. Simply put, we can definitely and realistically survive without them.

Now, before going any further, you have to know that this is not going to be an easy exercise. Doing without something that you need – or think you need – takes a lot of getting used to. It would take you a lot of effort, focus, and motivation. You would then need all the self-discipline that you can muster in order to succeed.

But, then again, that's what we're after, right?

The needs that we are referring to here are not your basic needs. Rather, these are the "other needs" or the ones that we think we can't live without but, in fact, (we) can.

Alright, it could be a little tricky figuring out which ones should go. So, feel free to refer back to *Maslow's Hierarchy of Needs*, and remember that part of self-discipline is being able to discern while staying true to oneself. Only you can determine what a basic need for you is.

Still confused? Here is a list of the things that people frequently mistaken for basic needs. Yes, they can be considered necessities, but cutting them out of your life will not eventually lead to death:

- ❖ (Your) Car – Walk instead of using a car, or just ride a bicycle. Aside from you getting some good exercise, you'll also learn better time-management by walking to work because you'd have to wake up earlier than usual.

- ❖ Mobile phones – You don't always need them. Your parents and grandparents survived without them, so why can't you? Furthermore, even if a lot of processes have been changed by this technology, it won't hurt to try doing without it. Remember, gadgets can take away a huge chunk of your time, energy, and attention – things that you should be spending really wisely.

- ❖ Extra cash – This is definitely not a need, and so is your credit card. You already know how bringing your CC (or extra amounts of cash) can tempt you to buy so much stuff, but you still bring them anyway. Everyone's favorite excuse? "Emergency." While this may be a valid excuse, using it to justify why we always need to have an excess might become a bad money habit that can lead to financial problems like overspending, racking up debts, etc. So, do yourself a favor. Resist the temptation to bring extra. Instead, fill your wallet with coupons, gift cards, and discount cards. They're a lot more helpful and they teach you the value of staying within your means.

- ❖ The Internet – Okay, this might be a little over the top. But, as you know, being online 24/7 is not only bad for your health – it keeps the mind stagnant as well. You see, having free access to a vast amount of information does not make you wiser or more knowledgeable. It merely gives you the information that you need to digest – not going anywhere but the drain. You won't learn yoga just by reading about it. You won't see Mt. Fuji just by staring at its pictures. The better thing to do is to go out there and experience life. Self-discipline is better realized and formed in actual scenarios, not in virtual worlds.

To deprive ourselves of such things would definitely build our character as it will force us to welcome a different kind of change – *elimination* – and such change often requires effort.

Now, if you really should have some of these things, due to health or employment reasons for example, then just set a realistic limit for yourself. Later on, you'll realize why less is more and develop a strong sense of self-discipline when it comes to eliminating the (often unnecessary) things we strongly believe we can't live without.

A Different Perspective on Failure

People say that failure is a catalyst for success. Understandably, though, no one ever wants to fail – not even if it meant being successful in the end.

Just like rejection, failure creates negative feelings. The only difference is that people and situations do not fail you, they reject you. You fail yourself – or you yourself fail.

As harsh as that may have sounded, that is the cold hard truth about failure. You determine your own failure (or success) and people do not have anything to do with it, though they could have an influence to some extent.

15. The Failure Exercise

Failure is sometimes better than rejection. Why? It is because you can do something about it. Also, looking at it from a different perspective, failure is somehow related to how you handle rejection.

A good example would be when applying for a job. Say you have been turned down for the tenth time in a few months. By now, your ego must already be so small that you even can't call it ego anymore. You balk at the feeling of being denied several times – unless of course you're a master of overcoming rejections (which we have already discussed).

But, then again, a "No" today might be a "Yes" tomorrow. True failure, in this case, means not trying again or not trying to learn what you keep on doing wrong so you can do something about it. Success is doing otherwise, and you must have already figured that out yourself.

Still, people actually stop trying out of their fear to fail miserably and hurt their ego even further. Again, this is quite understandable. Fear of failure is a valid, universal fear – but it is not impossible to overcome.

A simple exercise that aims to improve our sense of self-discipline through overcoming this fear requires that we subject ourselves to failure deliberately and repeatedly. But, just like the previous character building exercises (rejection therapy, cold conditioning), this activity is not meant to hurt us or to make it difficult for us without a greater purpose.

The failure exercise is actually a set of activities that you can do where success is less likely and failure is more imminent.

If you're a single guy, try to approach as many attractive single women as you could. For single ladies (this is going to be much more intimidating), do the same and approach as many attractive single men. Of course, not every interaction will result in good news, but that is the whole point. You'll be better at handling rejections and failure after this activity.

Note that this exercise (or therapy to some) is not requiring you to neglect your job or your family just to fail intentionally. All it is asking is that you try to befriend failure – to remove all of your negative first impressions and just go with it.

16. Embrace awkward situations

Discomfort is not always physical. Emotional discomfort can do wonders in helping you get exposed to adversity.

We've all been in an awkward situation at least once in our lives – awkward first kiss, mistaking a stranger for a friend, realizing you are in the wrong class, or laughing really hard while no one else is amused. The list goes on and our natural reaction is either to play it cool or to scamper away.

While it is not exactly failure, being in an awkward situation allows us to get a good laugh and, occasionally, teaches us to admit that we made a mistake or don't know what to do.

Try to put yourself in awkward situations and see how you do – it doesn't matter what the results are. What matters is the exposure.

17. Don't be afraid to ask

Ask questions especially if you are unsure of the answer. Ask for small things or favors, and eventually move on to bigger things. Allow yourself to become vulnerable and do not be shy to ask, especially if there is something that you really desire. Want your friends to try your product? Then go ahead, ask them.

Try going to a flea market or a used goods store and haggle. If they say "No", try to not take things personally. You may think that it is you that they rejected, but it is not. Look at it from a different perspective and then try again. How you will respond will determine your failure or success and, if you're lucky, then you just might get what you truly want in life.

Always staying on the safe side and within our comfort zones won't teach us to feel, understand, and cope with these feelings that are normally associated with failure. But, whenever we fail, we build certain traits and habits, and characteristics needed to become well-disciplined individuals.

As the saying goes, "Nothing ventured, nothing gained." This holds true when speaking about failure. Without trying and failing, we also fail to learn and grow.

18. Learn something new and difficult

This is also a kind of failure test. It exposes you to challenges. But more importantly, this allows your mind to go on active mode.

Learning to play an instrument in particular is a good move if you want to build self-discipline. The application and repetition as you learn to play the guitar, piano, flute, violin, or sax, will enhance your focus. You will reprogram your mind and improve your attitude. You will know that even if things are not easy, you can choose to do what is right and enjoy the benefits that come after. You will apply what you learn in what you do every day and you will develop good habits that bring you success

Try to learn a new language (or languages) or some new sports that are outside of your abilities.

Allow yourself to fail and be frustrated by not learning or becoming capable of what you have to. You'll become better at handling frustrations thereafter. Just don't be hard on yourself if you suck at your new endeavor.

19. Push Yourself to the Limit

Often, the best feeling of success comes from when we've decided to push ourselves to the limit – to the point of breaking – and eventually reached our goals.

However, it is also not so often that we try to peer into the void of our unknown abilities? Why? Because, *why should we?*

We work our jobs double-time and work really hard out in the gym, and we think of these as hard work because, indeed, they are. Still, they don't necessarily mean that we've pushed way beyond our comfort zone where our limits typically rest. Do we care at all, though?

Pushing through incredible amounts of physical and mental pain just don't usually fit into our daily lives and routines.

Furthermore, many of us have already submitted to the belief that such a challenge is only for "the great" (e.g. Thomas Edison who failed a thousand times but pushed further and invented the light bulb; Hillary and Norgay who both went through extreme pain and exhaustion before reaching Mt. Everest's peak).

Many people are as capable of pushing themselves past what thought to be their physical, mental, and even emotional limits. Here are the basic steps on how you can do so albeit at a smaller scale.

❖ Create a goal – Without any objective, you might not be challenged well enough. Oftentimes, a huge part of staying motivated to push through is the end goal. Furthermore, set a goal that is beyond what you think you are capable of or what you have accomplished so far.

❖ Push with small strides – Pushing past your limits doesn't always mean achieving big things all at once. It doesn't hurt to take baby steps so long as you are consistently making progress or working your way up. (e.g. better to slowly increase the weight rather than suddenly lift a significant amount of additional weights and then break). This part will also help build your tolerance for more.

❖ Challenge yourself further –Once you've felt like you already reached your limit, go one step more!

For example, your workout routine usually takes 12 reps of leg lifts. Why not try going for 14 this time? Of course, you should do this only when you're reasonably sure that it won't cause you any injury. You should know your limits as well.

Another example is applying for a position you feel you might not be the best candidate for. Of course, you should still be reasonable, but there's nothing wrong with shooting for a spot that is supposed to require 5 years' experience when you've only been in the field for 2.

Fear, doubt, physical inability, and a negative past are just some of the obstacles that might stop you from going above and beyond your own boundaries. But, you wouldn't know how far you can go if you won't even try pushing through them.

This exercise is meant to help you grow self-discipline by teaching you how to push past the discomfort when you seem to have met a point of resistance – your limits. It also teaches mental toughness or that which allows us have that "mind over matter" kind of attitude.

Today, you can do what you normally would – do the same activities, work the same job, and put the same level of effort.

Or... you can push yourself to do more and reach new heights.

Living with Intent and Purpose

Do you ever feel like being in several places all at once but not feeling fully present at the same time? Do you often fly from one place to another, feeling super, only to end up exhausted at night and to wake up to do the same things the next day?

Or it could be that you are too busy, too distracted to even notice your inner life passing you by...

You are not alone. Every day, various things capture our attention and we tend to get easily preoccupied. But, who could blame us? Distractions are a part of life and they come in many forms. Some are pleasant, some are not. Some are important for our living, while some are just time-wasters.

Either way, many of these things take away so much of our time and, as a result, gets the better of us. Busy schedules, social media, grocery lists, advertisements – there is just so much going on in our lives all at once.

To live with intent, on the other hand, is to allow ourselves to achieve a clear sense of mind so that we can become more present and, therefore, more aware of what is truly going on. It also aims to develop our sense of focus and self-control – key components of self-discipline.

Furthermore, by being in the here and now, we are able to reconnect with our inner selves and find peace and joy amidst the haste of everyday life. This part of the book will teach you some techniques as to how.

After all, wouldn't it be great if you could be capable of more meaningful life choices in this rat race that is called life?

20. Make Time for Quiet Moments

"The quieter you become, the more you are able to hear."

-Rumi

Effective self-discipline requires a lot of concentration. With everything that is going on around us, though, it is often challenging to maintain a sense of focus. The daily grind ultimately becomes our habit and then turns into a daydream from which we couldn't just snap out of.

Likewise, we become so caught up in haste that we already find it almost impossible to slow down (or stop), step back, and look at things from a better perspective.

Present moment awareness occurs after we've decided to become focused on the present by consciously removing distractions. This means that we need to be more mindful and to avoid overthinking – to have a clear mind to begin with. Present moment awareness is the core of purposeful living.

Achieving a sense of mental clarity, however, can be tough if the distractions are too strong that they result in sensory overload (e.g. too much moving, too much noise). How to deal? Make time for some peace and quiet:

❖ Quiet time at home – Allot a few minutes or few hours daily for some quiet thinking, reflection, internalization, or whatever you call it. Also, if you can, do it at the same time each day for it to become a routine.

Better yet, do it when and where none of the other people in the house can distract you, like in the shower or while enjoying a tub bath.

❖ Quiet time at work – Retreat for some quiet time in between meetings and presentations. It doesn't have to be that long – 5 to 10 minutes is just enough to allow you to reset. Spend these few minutes alone and without any distractions. Close the office door (if possible), go to a nearby park, or find your own quiet hideaway.

❖ Quiet time from media/social media – "Quiet" doesn't always mean the reduction of noise. You could spend some quiet time from certain things as well. In this exercise, you simply have to silence your email or social media accounts for several hours or even one whole day. Take a break from constantly checking them and rest your mind by "fasting" from news and current affairs.

Our world is getting noisier and noisier, but with enough commitment and creativity, it is still possible to achieve a daily dose of valuable silence.

21. Ditch Multi-tasking

Forget about what other people keep on telling you about multi-tasking. More often than not, it doesn't work and could end up doing more harm than good.

Sometimes, people resort to multi-tasking because they dislike the current task or are too anxious to complete multiple important tasks with looming deadline. It is almost always harmful because it is impossible to focus when working on multiple tasks. The quality of your work is hampered and you end up subjecting yourself to unnecessary stress. It also slows you down so you end up having to spend more time trying to complete a project.

22. **See Through the Tunnel Vision**

In ophthalmology, *tunnel vision* is the loss of peripheral vision caused by certain diseases of the eye such as glaucoma or retinitis. As the name implies, it is as if you are looking straight through a tunnel wherein your surrounding vision is dark and your focus is limited to what's in front of you.

In psychology, it means to have a narrowed, sometimes exclusive, focus on a certain emotion – same basic concept as the actual disease.

But how does having a tunnel vision help us in living a more purposeful and disciplined life?

Truth be told, a tunnel vision is not exactly a positive phenomenon both physically and psychologically. It is the opposite of effective situational awareness or broad perception. It is our tendency to focus on only a single point-of-view. In a nutshell, it is a negative mindset. Or is it?

On the subject of self-discipline, having a tunnel vision is actually beneficial. This is because temptations are less likely when there are fewer distractions. Also, a tunnel vision gives us a more focused perception and, thus, a better sense of self-discipline. This can be achieved in two simple steps:

- ❖ Slow down – Slowing down even for a few minutes allows us to focus on the present moment. But, we should be able to relax as well – no hurrying or worrying at this point.
- ❖ Become mindful – While mindfulness (training) has its own section for discussion, it is also an important step in this exercise. To become mindful, we must put all of

our attention on what it is that we need to focus on. A good example of this is when we are about to be late for work – either we skip breakfast or grab the first food that we see (which is usually unhealthy) and then go. But, applying mindfulness in this case will allow us to slow down a bit to think clearly, assess the situation more carefully, and take a more appropriate action.

Making use of our tunnel vision, especially in stressful situations, is a good self-discipline habit to develop. Aside from giving us the ability to slow down and focus on the problem without judging quickly, it also lessens the likelihood of us making emotionally-charged decisions and actions.

23. Use the Power of Visualization

It can be hard for some people who rarely take time to really envision their future. After all, we are here living in the "now".

What we fail to realize, though, is that by giving in to small, instant gratifications now, we are depriving our future self of the bigger and better rewards later.

Say for example, you've already envisioned yourself as someone fitter and more attractive 6 months from now, which is why you started a diet regimen in the first place. But, your family ordered 2 boxes of your favorite pizza, some chips which used to be your comfort food, and bottles of iced cold cola. Now, you are hungry and the summer heat is killing you. What would you do? A) Eat what your family ordered or B) Get something healthier

If this is an actual scenario, some people would have gone for option A because it is instantly rewarding. Likewise, some people would choose $100 now over $200 in a year or a pair of shoes today over two pairs of shoes in 6 months. People tend to want things now rather than later, which is common but not always the best choice.

In psychology, this is called "temporal discounting" or the phenomenon in which the subjective value of some reward loses its magnitude when the given reward is delayed. This is as opposed to the concept of "delaying gratification" which is important in self-discipline.

Going back to our example, what do you think your future self would have chosen?

Now that you've learned about the benefits of silence and of any conscious effort to remain focused and present, it is time to move a bit farther into the future using our minds.

The reason we're doing this is still because of intent – we are trying to lead a life of purpose. Conversely, without this purpose, we are simply going day to day without any real direction or focus, and lacking the self-discipline that we need to succeed.

You can never live life fully at the moment unless you consciously tap into your subconscious or the inner part of you where your dreams reside, and sometimes, it helps to spend quiet moments visualizing things instead of planning your next course of action.

Yes, just like how you would daydream, you have to visualize how you'd like to be seen or where you'll be weeks, months, or years from today. Just the mere thought of this activity sounds exciting. But then, this is neither a daydream nor a wish. You are to visualize your goal and this goal should be S.M.A.R.T. (specific, measurable, attainable, realistic, and time bound).

Remember, we are not trying to deviate from the reality. In fact, we are still supposed to be mindful of the present. We are merely going to take pictures of our goals using our minds.

So, be careful not to overthink. More importantly, make sure you'll remember the picture. Here's a sample scenario:

Envision yourself showing off your figure at the beach this coming summer. Imagine people staring in awe as you flaunt a hot pink bikini over your sexy body. Think about what your friends are going to say and how beautiful your pictures will turn out. Imagine being happy with the way you look and all the good times that you'll be having...

See? How's that for an end goal? You may even write down what you saw and keep it as a reminder of what you are trying to achieve. Doing so can certainly help you maintain your discipline.

The next time that you'll be setting a diet goal (for example), you can do this simple visualization technique. It is far better than simply having a goal "to lose weight" or to "lose 20 pounds".

Finally, do not hesitate to use the techniques that we already covered. Retreating to peace and silence, for instance, helps a lot in reducing distractions to a minimum while using your tunnel vision allows for better focus and, thus, greater mind pictures.

24. Let Future 'You' Give A Pep Talk

An effective way to keep you motivated and well-disciplined is to spend some time visualizing your desired results and end goal.

Even better, imagine what your future self – the one that you wish become – would say to the person that you are now.

One exercise that you can do is to write your present self a letter from the viewpoint of your future self.

Create a detailed vision of this person depending on the goals you're working on.

What is his job? Where does he live? Is he in a relationship? Does he own a house? What does he do to unwind after work? Be as detailed as possible.

Is he or she successful and happy, or the exact opposite? Either vision of this future self – good or bad – should have something to say. What is this person going tell you? What are you supposed to do?

By having a meaningful conversation with the future you, what is yet to come may feel more tangible. Future will cease to exist in virtual reality and it would be easier for you to think that it is here right now – that what you do today instantly shapes your future so you might as well do your best.

25. Keep a Compass of Values

In a fast-paced world like ours, it is often so easy to get lost in a cycle.

Constantly, there is a sea to navigate – a sea of dreams, a sea of goals, a sea of opportunities, etc. Life, therefore, is never stagnant water, especially for those who are trying to live their best. Instead, it is an ebbing tide – a good thing except for the fact that we can't always be sailing on smoothly...

Our navigation skills will relentlessly be put to test and we might even find ourselves lost in this big ocean called life. What can we do in such a scenario, then?

Enough of the metaphors, but there is indeed a tool that we can use – a compass – our *compass of values.*

Values are different from goals. You can never *reach* a value, but you can live in accordance to it. Often, when our goals seem too far away to reach, it is our values that see us through.

Furthermore, core values help us live with intent because these are the beliefs that we hold about what matters the most in our lives. Therefore, our values are also an important factor that determines how disciplined we can get. In fact, self-discipline is a value.

We must remember, though, that we have different sets of life values. We may value such things in life as challenges, achievements, and stability, while a close colleague may value family-love and selflessness instead. As Friedrich Nietzsche has defined it, "You have your way. I have my way. As for the right way, the correct way, and the only way, it does not exist."

That being said, we must build our own compass of values, if we haven't yet, to use as guide when we feel lost. Here's how to do it:

- ❖ Think of at least 4-5 core values – Set aside some quiet time to reflect on these. You can even use Reflective Meditation (discussed previously) in finding your answers.

- ❖ Prioritize your core values – List down the values and with #1 being the most important, assign them numbers 1, 2, 3... and so on. These 5 values are what you deem as the most important ones in your life – these are the core values of your compass.
- ❖ Write down your core values and keep them close – Last but not the least, jot down what you have created. This list will serve as your compass. Put it somewhere you can easily access, like your wallet, to read and re-read whenever life seems to be pushing you to the wrong path (e.g. threatening to destroy your sense of self-discipline when it comes to your work ethics or the diet that you just started).

Indeed, life can get too difficult to navigate that it can even lead us to directions we're not supposed to go. But, with a compass of values to guide our way, we can easily find our way back home.

26. The If-then Technique

If you're building self-discipline in order to get closer to your goals, making if-then plans is a solid planning tool. It works this way:

1. First, you establish a triggering point or situation.

2. Then, connect it with a concrete behavior.

That's why it's called the if-then technique. It allows you to train yourself to respond to certain situations despite what your feelings might be pushing you to do so.

This is an example of an if-then plan:

If people say something that I find offensive, I will take a deep breath and then count to 10 before responding.

Here are more examples:

If I'm going out for a meal, then I will choose a salad.

If the alarm clock goes off, then I will immediately get up and head to the toilet.

The if-then statement should be executed regularly though. Only constant practice will enable you to build the association between the trigger point and the concrete behavior that you want to exhibit.

This is also a great way to create patterns that could build your restraint. It can work so well that what you're working on could eventually be a habit – something that you could do on autopilot. So even when you're stressed at work, you aren't going to be snapping at the next person who makes a harmless comment about your desk.

27. Self–Monitor

Self-monitoring is a way to get feedback. It allows you to keep focused on the goals and in some cases, it can be a good source of extrinsic motivation.

When you track and analyze your progress, you will be able to tell if your actions are doing something to get you closer to your goal. Tracking your progress shows you when and how to change your direction or pace when it is needed.

It lets you see if you need to make a few more adjustments. It can also encourage you because it lets you see how far you have gone. Of course, it will allow you to measure how much you need to work on to achieve your goal. When you see the truth before you, you will not have any excuses and you will be more motivated.

Not only does it let you track your progress. It also helps you become an expert in recognizing your own behaviors. This awareness will allow you to be more capable of dealing with impulses and knowing your triggers.

Building Mental and Physical Fortitude
to Reinforce
Self Discipline

A healthy mind and body is a good foundation for self-discipline and vice versa. Therefore, our health and our sense of self-discipline are two interrelated entities.

After all, how can we be fit and healthy if we are not disciplined enough to maintain a proper diet, exercise or go to the gym, and make sure we are always well-rested? Likewise, how can we have the strength, energy, and willpower to keep ourselves disciplined if we are always sick and weak?

Remember, some of the exercises mentioned for character building need some bodily strength to be performed (e.g. cold tolerance, pushing to the limit). Whatever we do to our bodies affects the mind and whatever affects the mind affects our self-discipline. Thus, it is always best to have a healthy body and mind to begin with.

28. Practice Meditation

Meditation is a term that we often associate with words like relaxation, calmness, mindfulness, yoga, etc. In general, we see it as something that is positive for the mind. This is true. However, there is more to meditation than merely closing your eyes and assuming various yoga positions.

The meditative practice is a technique used for resting the mind that involves turning your attention to a single point of reference – a focus – which is actually the inner self. One of its goals is to attain a state of consciousness that is unlike the normal waking state, and eventually reach a higher level of awareness and clarity of the mind.

As discussed previously, to live with such intent is to have a clear mind and a sense focus – contributing factors to the development of self-discipline. Without these, however, we might find it hard to gain inner peace, better perception, and a sense of self-control. Therefore, meditation is one of the best practices that can help us achieve long term self-discipline by allowing us to live purposefully.

Still, there are other reasons why being meditative eventually results in becoming more self-disciplined:

❖ We stay clear-headed in stressful situations – Stress and pressure can sometimes make us lose our cool. This is because as humans, we tend to give in to instant gratification and to forget our long-term goals in the heat of the moment (e.g. lighting a cigarette or grabbing a bag of chips when stressed out). Meditation can help us be "in the moment" of clarity and discernment where our minds would eventually recognize the difference between a need and want.

❖ We tend to crave less and be happier – Whereas exercise is for the body, meditation is for the mind, and while exercising puts stress on the body, meditation helps us relax. They do have one similarity, though – they make us feel good! Studies show that just like exercise, meditating can stimulate the production of such bodily chemicals as dopamine and endorphins which limit urges and cravings, and bring about good mood.

❖ We develop stronger willpower – A 2009 Duke University-Caltech study showed how meditation is related to higher levels of willpower by analyzing the brains of 37 dieters, particularly the dorsolateral prefrontal cortex section. In other words, those who meditated demonstrated greater willpower over their cravings than those who did not, so they (ones who meditated) were also predicted to have higher success rates – and they really did.

Furthermore, there are various meditation types and techniques to choose from. We just have to know which one or what combination we'd like to practice regularly:

❖ Concentration Meditation – By the name itself, the emphasis of this type of meditation is on improving our concentration.
  o Subtypes: Zen Meditation, Transcendental Meditation, Chakra Meditation)
❖ Reflective Meditation – Also known as Analytical Meditation, this type requires that a question be chosen and analyzed or reflected upon (e.g. "Who am I?" or "What is my role in the universe?")
❖ Mindfulness Meditation – As one of the most powerful meditation techniques, Mindfulness Meditation has

been known to help provide physical pain relief and even helps in the treatment of anxiety and depression.

- o Deep Breathing Meditation, Mindful Breathing, Sitting Meditation Walking Meditation)
- ❖ Heart-Centered Meditation – This type of meditation focuses on loving kindness and compassion, and on the healing of hearts.
- ❖ Creative Meditation or Visualization – This type aims to cultivate and strengthen various qualities of the mind. (e.g. joy, patience, empathy, gratitude, humility, etc.)

In our pursuit to grow further in self-discipline, meditation is a great exercise to learn and make a habit of.

29. **Have an attitude of gratitude.**

Self-discipline is developed along with self-contentment. While it is not bad to desire some things, a lot of people waste time and effort on wanting more things. They focus on what they don't have yet instead of what they already possess and enjoy. Having an attitude of gratitude will cause you to shift your mindset. When you are thankful for what you have, you will be happier, you will be able to control your emotions, and you will have a clearer mind and a healthier spirituality.

When you do not focus on your lack, but instead on the abundance of what is before you, you will develop self-discipline which will empower you to achieve your goals. By being grateful, you will rid yourself of worry and fear. Being worry-free will greatly improve your health – you will be less stressed. When the body and mind is stressed as your mind is fixed on lack, cortisol, epinephrine, and other stress hormones are released and they affect different body systems unfavorably.

How do you develop an attitude of gratitude? Start by spending a few minutes everyday to think of and write down the things, people, and events that you're thankful for. Keep a journal to remind yourself of what you already have. This will reinforce the gratitude in your heart and mind. Remember, there is always something in life to be grateful for.

You can reinforce this attitude by saying gratitude affirmation statements and maintaining a gratefulness journal.

For the next 7 days, think of something you can be thankful about as soon as you wake up. A bed to sleep on? A roof above your head? Food on the table? Extra pillows, maybe? Being able to sleep in on a weekend?

Before you go to sleep, think of something that happened during the day that you are thankful for. There are many things to be grateful about – find one, write it down and think about it. It will make you happier and more content.

30. Take care of yourself

When you don't eat well or sleep enough, your judgments and capacity will be impaired. Self-disciplined people know that this can hamper self-control. They know when to stop and rest. They know to eat well, sleep enough, and make healthful choices when it comes to exercise and compliance to medication or treatments. They know how to manage stress. Previous sections of this book provided some starter guides for stress management and creating a plan which you may apply to drafting your own our workout plan.

The other important aspect is diet. Things constantly get in the way of us maintaining a healthy diet – various stressors, our busy work schedules, getting preoccupied with social media, etc. There are just too many distractions and temptations around us.

What we should focus on, hence, is maintaining our sense of self-discipline when it comes to eating healthy because whatever food we eat greatly affects the neurochemical processes of our brain – bodily processes that are important for the mind-body connection. How to, then?

Manage your stress properly. Whenever we are stressed out or feeling pressured, we tend to compensate by reaching for the easiest pleasure that we could find and, most often, it is food – usually unhealthy ones. Thus, stress management is also an important part of eating healthy. Some good ways to deal with stress include relaxation techniques, exercise (releases happy hormones), and meditative practices. At all cost, resist the urge to reach out for food first.

Prioritize having healthy food that makes you feel full faster – The fuller our stomachs feel the less likely we are to eat more. Foods that can make us feel full faster and longer include high-fiber foods, water-rich vegetables, nuts etc. Avoid too much fat and carbohydrates, though these can also give a sense of fullness.

31. Forgive yourself and keep moving forward.

Keep in mind that on the road to developing this behavior, you will experience challenges which can either bring you amazing success or devastating failures.

There will be times that you'll fail at self-discipline. Sometimes, you give in, and sometimes, you fail to meet your deadlines.

You may have overspent last week. You may have slept in and didn't go to the gym as scheduled. You may have lost your cool and shouted at someone.

You will feel frustrated when things don't go as planned, and that's understandable. Failures can cause you to be angry at yourself, be frustrated or feel guilty.

But when you choose to spend your days in such a state, your life will go downhill. When you forgive yourself, you learn to let go of certain things. By acknowledging where you failed, you can identify the cause, learn from it and get going. Regardless of the ups and downs of your journey to enhancing self-discipline, you have to forgive yourself and carry on. Life can hit you hard, but you need to get back up and pursue a positive direction. It's not about how hard you fall, but how fast you get back on track. The longer you stay down, the harder it will be for you to grow and achieve success.

When you forgive, you learn to let go, and in that process, you actually end up regaining control. That is how the habit of forgiveness helps you achieve self-discipline. It allows you to let go of negativity and unnecessary anxiety, and refocus on how to remain the master of your own self.

32. Multi-Principle Training a.k.a. Interval Training

This technique will allow you to make use of multiple techniques – from making use of discomfort to timer training, stress management, and mindfulness to giving yourself a break.

1. Acknowledge that there is a need for you to commit to a task – and it's for your own good. It's a step to your ultimate goals.

2. Set the task to focus on for the training exercise -- be that working out, meditation, yoga, or writing.

3. Set the timer. We recommend 10 minutes. You can go for 5 minutes if you've yet to start building self-discipline and you think that 10 minutes is too long.

4.Option A: Start the timer and do the one thing you're supposed to do – embrace the discomfort.

4.Option B: Just sit there and don't do anything. Be kind to yourself if you can't bring yourself to do it.

5. When the urge arises for you to do something other than the set task, acknowledge the thought but refuse to do anything about it.

6. When the timer goes off, give yourself a break. You can do anything at that period, but only for 5 minutes.

7. Repeat the process.

You need to do this activity often in order to build discipline and mindfulness. You can start pushing yourself to the limit by gradually adding a minute to step 3 as you practice this technique.

Conclusion

Thank you again for purchasing this book!

I hope this book was able to help you to see the importance of learning, developing and improving your self-discipline so you can win in life. You have learned the many ways in which you can make small changes in your life to create not just a habit but a lifestyle of discipline.

The next step is to apply the concepts that you have learned from this book to make those small changes that will improve your focus and productivity. You can build your inner strength. Start small and start today. There is no one who can instill self-discipline in your life but you, and you will reap the benefits of this inner strength in every area of your life.

You are made for success in life – believe it, live it.

Believe it because doing so will reinforce your feeling of self-control and allow you to function better.

Today is the beginning of the best days of your life!

Jealousy

7 Steps to Freedom from Jealousy, Insecurities, and Codependency

Introduction

The story of jealousy dates way back into the early times of mankind. When people were not able to transcribe emotions, mythology kicked in and gave a boost with two passionate tales.

In ancient Greek mythology, the goddess Athena was known as the goddess of weaving. In light of this knowledge, Athena believed herself to be the supreme in that design league. And hence, when she heard that a farm girl called Arachne was a better weaver than her, she was jealous. Arachne was at the hands of a goddess, and Athena challenged her to a contest of spinning. In spite of her status, Athena lost, and in a spiteful rage ruined Arachne's work. Out of self –pity, Arachne hanged herself.

Athena was wrought with guilt and decided to turn Arachne into a spider.

Until today, when you walk along any dark corner, or through a grimly lit alley, you will find spiders still weaving.

Not one to have one talent, Athena was also the goddess of battle and wisdom. She was born in the most spectacular way; out of Zeus' head fully dressed for war. You see, quite often Zeus would sleep with many women, and his wife, Hera, the goddess of marriage and childbirth, would grow truly jealous and deal with the women with whom Zeus broke the rules of their marriage with.

As seen in the two tales, jealousy knows no bounds. Man or God, it breaks the chains of choice and affects any living being. Luckily or unluckily (you get to choose), jealousy doesn't follow one to the grave.

Or maybe, it does?

Chapter 1: What Is Jealousy?

It is that eight letter word we all have an inclination to walking away from. Some love it. Some hate it. Some embrace the power of it. In a word, it can make or break a foundation that has withstood and weathered the storms for years, and just because of a few actions are done out of spite and without thinking.

Jealousy isn't a pleasant word to use either. In many communities, it is frowned upon, though it can be used to spark a relationship in tatters (we shall look further into this later on). It is among the bottom half of all the words used to describe an emotion, the kind of emotion that leaves one in tears and feeling emotionally tired. Therefore, it can be said that jealousy is an emotion that erupts to be used negatively or positively when in want of something or someone owned or loved by someone else. In this case, we shall refer to jealousy between people and things.

It is not to be confused with envy either, dear reader. I'm sure that was where you were headed but cool your boots. Envy is described rather efficiently as "the resentful or unhappy feeling of wanting somebody else's success, good fortune, qualities, or possessions". You see, envy is closely similar to jealousy but different in the sense of what that feeling is gauged towards.

Even though jealousy can be quite a painful emotional experience, well resourceful psychologists deem it as an emotion that begs to be noticed- as a wake-up call to action, to save a treasured relationship in danger of becoming obsolete, and measures need to be taken to take back the affection of a loved one. In this regard, jealousy is an important emotion, as it conserves social bonds, and motivates people to engage in etiquette that maintains a significant connection. It only depends on how well it is handled and manipulated into doing good and not turning it into a physically forceful tool.

An example always places things into wider perspective. Let's say a bloke named John finds out his girlfriend Jenny has a nerdy best friend called Tom, and she is cozying up to him in ways that he finds uncomfortable, and in ways that she doesn't to him. Now we cannot say that John is envious of Tom, but he is way jealous of him. However, in the case John had the amazing computer and sleek DJ skills; it would be wise to say that Tom is envious of John.

There are several misconceptions surrounding jealousy, and this book would prefer setting those myths in order. It is high time for the facts to be laid down properly with no stones left unturned, to uncover the who, what, when, where, why, and how of jealousy. It is believed by many to be a purely negative emotion, but for the most part, it is not. It is wholly natural, and should not be seen as a beast that arose from eating too much gluten or trying out a different hair conditioner. It is purely a part of our DNA, and it proves a healthy relationship. Without it, without that fear of losing a loved one means we do not care. This breed of jealousy isn't what hurts relationships, but its companion, nay, and sibling, obsessive jealousy, does.

The second myth is that jealousy takes off the steam in a relationship. What this implies heavily is that jealousy finds a way to bring back the zest in a relationship, particularly a romantic one. It's a little bit tricky to generalize the individual reactions to a jealous significant other, and therefore, a little spice of an ingredient called jealousy can strip away the complacency heavily found in most long term relationships and serves a cold reminder never to take a partner for granted. As I said earlier, a little jealousy is a spice, more like chili. It can serve as a major turn on.

When we are in a relationship, we have the strong belief that our significant other should not talk or hang out with other guys/girls, now in this one, most of us are guilty as charged. This kind of belief is a heresy! In a healthy relationship, there should be support and encouragement to make friends of any gender outside the relationship and keep them. However, boundaries should be set in such a manner as to convey respect, but both partners should have fulfilling friendships with other people.

This one goes into the nasty obsessive kind. Going through your partner's phone and social media is NOT okay. It is the exact opposite of all that are good and normal in a relationship. In any normal and working relationship, whether long distance or one in which you are so close to each other that you can hear them breathing at night, talk about your feelings. There is a sense in approaching your significant other in an open conversation rather than a confrontation.

Only the morals can be challenged with this one- not trusting your significant other, who has had priors in cheating when they say they are being faithful. It is quite natural for you to be hurt by dishonesty, but it is unjustified to use their past against them. Trust is something we choose to give, and it is quite unfair to both parties if one of you clearly doesn't trust the other. If it comes to the point of asking yourself if you trust your partner, always consider what it would take for them to earn your trust back. If the answer falls back on calling or texting them to see what they're up to, trust levels are really low there. If it so happens that your answer is to re-check yourself and adjust your attitude and etiquette, then a healthy relationship might bloom after all.

When an occurrence such as your partner being jealous of other people talking to you, and you find yourself thinking that it is protection they're offering, think again. Healthy relationships include healthy friendships. If your significant other tells you not to talk to other people, then that is a sign of bad faith- they do not trust you. It is an assertion of power and control, which can turn ugly and even abusive.

Seventh myth busted (boy, we are on a roll today!) - Jealous people carry the insecurity bug. Not the ladybug, but the dark cloud hovering over them - making them feel that they are being cheated on even if they are not. Being jealous is primal instinct, and in its own way, it's all about being in touch with our own emotionality. Forget about the crossed elbows and not-talking-to-each-other-scenario. A jealous partner who is aware of it may be meekly appreciative of the importance of their significant other to them. Clearly, we live in a world of a sea of change, a world where stability with family or workplace relationships or durability are all smoke and mirrors. A partner is an irreplaceable star.

Onwards and upwards I always say. Another myth is that jealousy leads to unruly behavior. It doesn't have to be implied like this, but it becomes a problem when someone doesn't know how to handle the emotions brought along by jealousy. We as human beings have the brains and power to make choices and control emotions.

Finally, the last misconception is that it is wrong to share feelings of the green-eyed monster with your partner. Nay I say, nay! Deep and meaningful love flourishes on transparency, honesty, and vulnerability. By opening up and saying what you truly feel emotionally, you are in actual fact saying that you care about your partner and would not know how to live with yourself if you lost such a precious part of your life.

It is quite troubling to find that an occurring ideology with people in general that it is a sign of strength and character to hide our insecurities and fears- put on a mask if you will. This common knowledge can perpetuate unfathomable heavy damage. It destroys true self-esteem and lays our relationships to waste.

Wisdom is realizing that acting strong is still acting. At times, we all really pretend to be something we're not, we leave our true selves in the dark and put on a mask. This, as common belief puts it, is done in an effort to control what we aspire others to think of us. Ergo, we camouflage and hide our true selves to seek the admiration of others when trying to avoid their displeasure and when we betray do this, we are only betraying ourselves.

Human beings obtain self-esteem from the relationship with our own selves. Manipulating our personality to gain recognition from others leads to a term called other-esteem as it does not come from the inside. The more we look for approval from others, the more dishonest we become with ourselves. The end result will drastically affect us and lead us away from authentic self-esteem. Clearly, this is the polar opposite of the actions we should be taking- embracing and holding on to our vulnerability. What vulnerable in this sense of the word means is frankness. This does not allow you to twist it to mean fragile or weak. Human beings experience emotions that make us feel like an open wound ready to be attacked again, emotions such as insecurity, doubt, and fear. In truth, these are valid emotions, however, due to our twisted and deluded ethnic expectations that demand the face of strength, we decide to mask these feelings from each other. This, in turn, leads to us living our lives falsely thinking that our inadequacies are unique to us, and forget that others go through the same sense of fear that we feel.

Wearing a mask to hide your true self to the world is what entails you being breakable. Accepting who you are as a person makes your strength reverberate from you and echo out into the void. It never matters what other people think of you. Never. Only your thoughts and actions matter, for now, and ever more. This is the highway to a normal and powerful anchor in your self-esteem.

Nobody wants to be judged. That is understood. However, becoming an introvert and finding your way into unhealthy hobbies such as writing creep comics in the dark web to satisfy the need to be appreciated (and finding out that the only readership you have is anonymous individuals living in their mother's basement) is neither helpful nor beneficial.

The moment one accepts themselves as they are with their flaws and ugly scars, that is the time to realize that there is no point in hiding your true self to the world, and this is what constitutes a strong core in morality. Embracing the fears and judgment you expect from the outside world and turning them into your strengths, that's what living is all about.

The only one who can judge you is your inner self. No one else has that right, well, unless you find yourself in a criminally inclusive situation. That, my friend, is a charge you will have to face, a jury of your peers.

A common term is self-abuse, which means the ability to inflict emotional pain on oneself by using the pain from the actions of others upon you. Avoiding the hurt of inflicting judgment upon yourself is the whole point of you reading these words, and to learn how to maintain a level of pride in your personal achievements, however little or inconvenient to you.

Remember always, that you are one in a seven billion (and soon to be eight million!), so quit judging yourself, quit listening to other's advice about who you are as a person and quit comparing yourself to other people.

Think of carrying an egg in your purse for months believing it to be a perfect incubator for it, but you end up with a naughty smell wafting through during an important meeting at work. Similar to that reference being made in light of a sense of comprehension that might not be there.

It is pointless.

It is a game of madness that we keep playing with ourselves, a game in which we shelve away the very qualities that make us special and unique in our loved ones' eyes and that make us more powerful than we could ever fathom.

The game needs to change.

Chapter 2: Types of Jealousy

There are two cases of jealousy, most common to the human race; reactive jealousy and suspicious jealousy. The difference is uncannily necessary, as almost everyone feels reactive jealousy when one assumes that their significant other is cheating, though people vary their inclinations to feel suspicious jealousy in the lack of any real risk. In both forms, a lot of hurt can take place in the relationship and once words are flung, they can never be taken back.

In describing the two cases one at a time, reactive jealousy, as it clearly ascribes to its name, is the type in which action takes place and not the kind in a cool sci-fi film. It's a survival and primal instinct humans have encoded in their DNA; to react to perceived danger to their loved ones.

When describing suspicious jealousy, it is in regard to a lack of evidence in foul play in the relationship. It occurs when one party in the relationship feels that there is a threat about to come into the relationship, but there is nothing to show for it but cold shoulders and rolled eyes. A case study example could be a simple wink or a smile or a flick of the hair from the lady in the television to your partner while watching Family Feud, and you feel a little bit uneasy from that. This might be a little overboard and dip into paranoia which shall be tabled in this chapter, but it is one that is based on senseless falsehood.

These two cases of jealousy are further split, and are a little bit of each other emotionally but wholly different with the scenarios in tow. Let's go into the details, shall we?

Normal Jealousy

a) Workplace jealousy - Jealousy in the workplace arises between colleagues competing for the same type of position, especially when a promotion comes up. Though at times it can be deemed healthy competition, some ethics to be considered in the workplace are usually not put into play. Workplace jealousy can get quite rough as competitors go for the jugular in order to get that salary raise. If one colleague feels that another received, but was unworthy of, a salary increase or a title promotion, they may experience jealousy. They may feel especially jealous if they felt that they worked more diligently to earn accolades that were only given to the other person, and also when the appreciation of effort made is lacking. Often, this creates a feeling of disappointment and jealousy in the heart of an employee.

b) Sibling rivalry - Members of a family normally compare themselves to one another. The universal form of family jealousy is sibling rivalry, which affects brothers and sisters of all ages. There is a general sense of competition amongst children to be their parents' favorite child. It is a case of instinct and devotion to the parents in question. Siblings may compare their successes with one another, contest for the most of their parents' affection, and struggle to play with the same toy. There is also a display of jealousy on the arrival of a newborn and being made to share most of their toys with them. In layman's terms, it's a situation that can be a real pain in the neck. Sibling rivalry can be felt in an instance where one sibling is more successful than the other in school or career, but it may also be undergone if one sibling has a disability that requires extra attention from other family members. The comparison between siblings also brings a divide between the children.

c) Romantic jealousy- This is the one in which we all can agree to have experienced at one point in our lives. It leaves one with raw pain and a nasty taste in one's mouth. When two people come together and make the choice to be in a relationship together, even the slightest inkling of a perceived threat to the relationship can cause serious implications such as breaking up, or in cases where partners are mental, physical distress. This is where the term schizophrenia and delusion come to call.

d) Platonic jealousy - This is the special kind of jealousy that arises in friendships due to the same insecurities found in other relationships; the feelings of judgment, a fear of being substituted, and feelings of competition. Two female friends may discover that they are attracted to the same man and claim that neither will "go" for him. Nonetheless, they may both begin to feel all three jealous insecurities concurrently; they may feel competitive to earn the man's attention, insecure about their individual abilities to win him over, and fearful that the man will ultimately act as a friend replacement. In most cases, this kind of distrust may be confused with romantic kind of jealousy, but it should be remembered that there is a fine line between the two emotions. Tight bonds with friends can be so glued together that one party cannot see their lives moving forward without the other.

d) Abnormal jealousy - It is an unjustified kind of a jealousy caused by no possible reasons except for psychological issues such as hallucinations, obsession, or schizophrenia. Under some extreme cases of abnormal jealousy, a person is known to display immaturity and insecurity as well as a controlling vibe. Such people tend to assume that their family members, friends, and partners are unfaithful to them. This kind of jealousy is usually described with words like gruesome, compulsive, or apprehensive. It can be accredited to extreme immaturity, insecurity or an obsession with being in control. Sometimes it is due to a mental illness such as schizophrenia or paranoia or caused by a chemical imbalance in the brain. This is mostly referred to as delusional jealousy in learned and medical circles.

In 1991, a bright fellow named Gerrod Parrott claimed that the clear distinction between all these levels of jealousy is the kind of threat imminent to that said relationship. In other words, what he meant was that for you to know which level of jealousy you are in, it would be a wise choice to clearly understand the level of perceived or real threat that will attack your relationship. If the occurrence of a threat is justified and there is solid proof of foul play in the relationship, then it can be truly said to be rational and precautions should be taken for it not to be reactive. However, if the claims of jealousy are only by imagination and cannot hold water in any way, then the only threat is imagined and can only result in suspicious jealousy.

Finally, the long hurdle of the types of jealousy comes to a halt. Several if counted one by one, but it's necessary to understand the different situations that may arise significantly in daily life. Be it a barbecue session with the family, workplace event, church group, or even prize giving day at school. Coming to terms with the level of jealousy you are in is a brave step in coming clean and healing the relationship severed.

Now you are in the know of the categories as they are with different types of relationships, with some familial and others professional. All in all, the effects and consequences are real, and we shall look further into this in the coming chapters.

Chapter 3: Self-Esteem and Jealousy

The two flow in the same river streaming in the same direction, and can collide if not steered properly away from each other. A new study conducted and published in Addictive Behaviors found out that people who depend on their relationship for self-esteem most commonly turn to alcohol once the green-eyed monster hits them and hits them hard. The research is the initial study to show the correlation between romantic jealousy, relationship-dependent self-esteem, and alcoholism. That was a mouthful, but in clear layman's terms, this means the link between steamy jealousy, clingy relationships with the result of low self-esteem, and nectar of the gods. The researchers from the University of Houston say that understanding the link between these three factors could help identify people at risk of alcoholism.

Different people deal with their stress in different ways, some run, some hit walls, others write it out, and few scream into the pillows and sleep it off. None of us is the same as the other. For some people, alcohol is go-to for pain relief. Don't get me wrong, a glass of the good stuff is fun and splendid with a friend after a hectic day at the office and shared with limits, but using it to deal with emotions is hard enough as it is.

Jealousy between two lovers is an event most couples would not appreciate experiencing, and an underlying issue is how little work has been put into researching how abuse of alcohol is related to it. Luckily, a study was done to demystify the correlations between these three. Studies prior to this one only researched on the link between alcohol abuse and jealousy, and therefore this was the first one to link the three- self-esteem, jealousy, and alcohol rage-together.

So, the buddies of high science and philosophy at one University gathered a group of 277 volunteers, of whom 241 were women (clearly women are more responsive to their emotions than men, hence the bulge in number), and asked them questions about their self-esteem issues with regard to how high it relies on their relationships on and off campus.

As expected, the ones with clingy issues to their relationships and their partners often turned to alcohol to deal with these emotions. For the participants who were in a state of buzz kill and non-activity to advance in what they were currently doing in their relationships with their partners, this was true.

Alcohol seemed to be used in high levels when suspicion arose in relationships. If a partner felt or imagined their partner cheating, they turned to alcohol for some numbing or courage to confront them about it.

Another study was conducted at Pennsylvania State University by a certain curious psychology professor named Jeffrey Parker. Parker researched the benefits of intimacy between children and their close friends, in order to understand levels of intimacy that are coupled with vulnerability, which may prove a relation between pessimism and jealousy.

The team at Penn University led by Parker assessed almost 500 5th to 9th graders who had some documented issues with themselves and others, issues pertaining to jealousy. This was done to achieve comprehension of teenagers' weaknesses and susceptibilities to jealousy.

A series of questions was designed for 27 willing volunteers (for no pay at all, which was very mature of them if I do say so myself). What was found in the questions was very peculiar and increasingly interesting as they went by, questions assessing how the volunteers felt when their best friends chose someone else to go shopping with or do an activity without involving them.

Beyond the scope of this study that was divided into two parts, the researchers questioned the volunteers' popularities for being ones to hold a grudge on a classmate by asking their peers at school to evaluate them.

This is what the study found out;

Those girls (not too obvious, huh?) held the reputation of high jealousy levels than boys. This is because girls tend to expect affection (kindness, care, and an occasional carrying of their books all day) in their friendships more than boys did.

It was also found out that girls became more aggressive when it came to dealing with hormones. In this case, they shoved more and hurled really mean words to others if things didn't go their way. However, both boys and girls were both passively and actively aggressive when jealous.

Both girls and boys pointed out their jealousy tendencies to being lonely and not having someone to talk to and air out what they are going through.

Most teenagers have an irrational fear of disloyalty and unfaithfulness in their relationships when they decide to have them, with this, fear of being replaced by their friends is high. Hormones and high levels of caffeine and activity during the day tend to lead to this.

It was noted down that most teenagers have an inability to hold their friendships and relationships for a long period of time due to the fear of being replaced, leaving them feeling lonely and unapproachable on the inside.

Way past the times of modernism and free thinking, people thought that jealousy was a high case of being strong and having a high self-esteem. Yet the fairer sex has been proving it time and again that jealousy is a true sign of low self-esteem, especially in the dawn of the 21st century.

Does this theory make any semblance close to the truth?

Yes.

It really does.

Jealousy is a real sign of truly having a low self-esteem, and in the following chapters, there are certain remedies for that bad case of the green. Finding yourself in those chapters is bravery only for the few.

It is with high hope that the research done will help you, dear reader, to manage and knowing how to enslave the end results might be for you if it ever comes to the point of high alcohol consumption because of an emotion unfounded and constructed with fear and instability in a relationship.

It is important to note that jealousy and low self-esteem are in no way the same. One can inflame the other and fuel it to ridiculously high levels. The difference in both emotions is how you deal with them, positively or negatively, for which the ultimate choice solely lies in your hands.

Chapter 4: Why Are You Jealous?

A tinge of jealousy in a relationship is natural and at times described as healthy. Funny isn't it, that a thing that could break down the strongest of relationships to its knees is regarded as healthy. In several countries all over the world, jealousy is a matter that the older generation laughs about with each other as it is an emotion they learned to deal with over the years, and only the youth find it a milestone to take it by the horns. All over the world, jealously brings relationships to their knees in regards to being heated over if they are not. That tiny tweak of jealousy in a relationship is a feeling most people can relate to. We all feel that bout of jealousy due to the sense of losing that special connection we have with someone and he/she might find someone to replace us. Most people feel it on very few occasional basis, while there are those special collections of people who feel it to an unreasonable standard.

Well-established psychologists and scientists in kind over the decades have taken their time to study the origins and effects of jealousy. In some cases of research, it was found out in 2004 that jealousy may have a physical connection to the body differently in the genders.

To be more accurate, in 1995 it was decided that there is a specific layer of circuitry in the brain that encompasses jealous reactions, and discovered men were overcome by jealousy about a physical adultery, while women were hurt more by emotional perfidy (in as much as most men deny this fact, it is very true on all levels).

What follows in the next few statements is why you might find yourself jealous, and if you find that you relate to most of the situations, know that you are not alone.

Insecurity

Undoubtedly, this is the one that gives most relationships the shivers when thought of. The term inferiority complex is commonly used to reflect the primarily damaged self-esteem of a partner who is conflicted with jealousy.

It is intriguing to note that people in power, leaders, politicians, and those who hold office in authoritarian roles are not exclusive of this mentality. It gets to anyone anywhere, and since it feeds on love and hate at the same time, it finds itself quite the meal in almost every household.

Compulsive thinking

It is common for those who are diagnosed with OCD (obsessive-compulsive disorder) not to understand why their partners would cheat on them, let alone comprehend the feelings of jealousy. However, their brains tend to function compulsively into overdrive, and this is the case for clingy types of people. Anyone diagnosed with the disorder can confess to you how difficult it is to manage the fear of the unknown. They can come up with the oddest of stories about their partner's infidelity, completely unfounded and based on suspicion.

A case of distrustful personality

Paranoia is as severe as you would believe. Don't let it fool you; it can arise from the smallest of issues, even those which are as meaningless as going to browse on the toilet with your phone. Since it takes the form of schizophrenia in many circumstances, the high number of individuals diagnosed with this mental case lie on the less noisy side of this battlefield.

Several people in relationships today have some paranoia in short bursts, but not in the severity of the real disorder in its own right. Mild paranoia in couples or relationships proves great difficulty in having trust with one another. Quite often, they perceive lies and firmly believe in treachery in the relationships they have.

Reality smacks you in the face with a glove.

Ask a child with crumbs all over their faces if they ate the cookies and they will give you so many reasons as to how the cockroaches and rats came into the house and took them away and ran off on holiday before they got them.

Long story short, a jealous person will defend themselves when asked why they were jealous. It could be a series of incidences or just one remote incident. It is fair to place labels on a person who has had serial cases of jealousy as a jealous person by default if they cannot justify their claims of cheating.

When it so happens that there is no prior case to jealousy with you in your previous relationships, then the case of current jealousy in your relationship is not problematic. You're just being worried and apprehensive, and this is natural and should not make you feel belittled.

In conclusion, jealousy holds one hostage most times when felt, even when you know it does not make sense. Most people could go so far as to say jealousy is a companion in troubled storms, a friend to hold at the end of the world. To be fair and true, jealousy is an emotion to be felt whether we want to or not.

It is a great show of maturity to overcome innate feelings of jealousy. Understanding how the connection between you and your partner resonates is a way to swerve through the murky waters of suspicion and infidelity and rise above into the light of commitment and trust.

A relationship without jealousy holds no spark, no passion, and no divine bond that keeps the connection eternal. If there is no jealousy then it means you are a vampire- being able to switch off emotions like a light bulb whenever you want, and that hunger to be together no longer exists.

All over the world several communities have labeled jealousy as a natural reaction between loved ones when something revered is tampered with, say communication within the household. This is where universal truth got it all wrong. Jealousy is part of being human, and you have to embrace it.

Social norms dictate some very queer rules. Men feel biologically favored to have several female counterparts, and society backs them up. They are actually patted on the back for cases of infidelity in most cultures, but for women to be in the same position, society curses them out as outcasts and women of low self-respect.

Why?

The world is a weird place, that's why.

With all the rules dictating that for two people to get married the 'arrangement' has to be conceded by a judge and have witnesses to assess the proof of that 'arrangement' is utterly preposterous. When it also comes to the unfortunate case of marriage not working out, divorce has to be overseen by a judge and in both instances; the government has to know the things going on with this issue. A real Big Brother no one ever asked for, right? And in all these, you cannot do it yourself, at all.

Tagging of labels onto something as divine as a relationship brings to light the unnecessary nature of it all. 'Sweet' tags such as, "Till death do us part", "She is mine", "Don't you dare touch my man", "I own that girl", are so wrong, and are some of the reasons and causes of jealousy.

If all this is considered into current relationships, you may find why jealousy creeps into them by default. The truth of the matter is the only person whose actions you are truly in control of is yourself and no one else. All those self-help books telling you how to 'keep your man' or 'never letting her go' or 'how to make sure she can't wait to see you after work' will not work. Separation can and will happen at any time, and not remedying the cracks in the wall will end the relationship without a moment's notice.

Looking deep into the matter of roots of jealousy, the following are some of the reasons, mostly theories, as to the origins of the emotion in various relationships:

1. Biologically speaking

a.) Regarding sexual and romantic jealousy

Reproduction is a strong motivator for people to keep on surviving in this world. Not only is it fun practicing having children, but also the drive to be overprotective over 'their' women (see what I meant with the labels?). The need to reproduce and sire the next generation means the birth of jealousy when the chance of a mate being stolen by another arises.

Thinking from a female point of view, which in this case puts things in greater perspective, being cheated on means that her mate slacks in providing the basic needs for her, and his infidelity, in turn, means fewer assets for her and her offspring.

That went a little Neanderthal, but is relevant even today.

b.) In terms of the things of this earth

A material possession being prized over by human beings is uncommon to none. We like shiny bits, and we know that at specific moments in life these things mean our survival. It is therefore not common to find jealousy surrounding the lack of availability and loss of certain material wealth. This is linked to superior genes, and in this case, the term survival of the fittest must definitely be used.

We always want to win in everything. It is just primal and there is nothing to really do about it. It can even be seen in children as they get a new toy or game of cards. They throw a tantrum when they lose and run around naked when they win.

All this is linked to us wanting to survive better and longer.

2. Onward to the mind waves and their expanded complexities (Psychologically speaking in case that went a tad too far)

From an educated point of view, the Maslow's Hierarchy of Needs is a pyramid that was designed by a famous psychologist, Abraham Maslow. It indicated that human beings are in the need for good self-esteem. The only real chase in life is the pursuit of happiness (yeah, quote me), yet people are always on the lookout for fleeting highs and things unnecessary to living. The thing that most people do not realize is that anything that lowers your self-esteem in the case can be ripped away from you instantaneously without the bat of an eyelid. Happiness and other valued qualities of a good life that make sense to everyone last the longest in relation to time.

Many parts of the world live this way, unfortunately, planning on how to get more rates or high investment portfolios, and this line of thought is encouraged by the capitalist movement in several parts of the world.

There are several other things that we detach ourselves from to make room for things that have no real meaning to us. The latter describes how much wealth one owns, how many friends one has, or how many people hold us dear to their hearts. Now, these are the things that leave us empty and void once they are all stripped away from us in a fleeting second. They are all smoke and mirrors and have no place in defining who we are as a person.

When one feels they have high self-esteem because of these material possessions, they are blatantly lying to themselves. Only the ego is being fed, and not the Freudian kinds of ego, mind you. This is the ego that blinds a soldier going into war only to kill them in the waking process. These possessions make you feel so good about yourself, and they never want you to let them go. The devil's deal you see. The more you hold on to them, the more 'fulfilled' you feel.

This is where and how jealousy comes into play in this. Coupling yourself with these fleeting highs births jealousy as a byproduct. In the defining moment where you find yourself close to losing these material possessions, heavy negative emotion washes over you. The fear of loss is a powerful one, and this might be why people have a strong reaction while trying to catch the wind; the wind, in this case, is the material wealth.

How to deal with this materialism:

> You've already taken the first step. Acknowledging you have a problem is the first step. Second, you are already aware that self-worth is more important than placing value in materialistic ventures.

Always ask yourself, if the materialistic ventures were not there, would you still feel good or even great about yourself? Plainly being alive and existing in this world is enough to make you worth something, and just as equal to anything valuable in the world.

Your value is placed on the good things you can do in this world and how amazing your contribution, be it magnanimous or so small it cannot be seen, can be.

Keeping this as a constant reminder can go a long way in improving your self-esteem, your self-worth, and seeing the worth in others as well. All the joy and laughter and music and wonder all depend on whether you decide to let all the materialism go and embrace your true inner self with no chance of reward or witness. In the words of Andy Dufresne, "They can never take what is in your mind. What's there is yours forever."

b.) Who you are as a person being put in the same category with random achievements.

There is a certain unspoken rule of thumb in never associating feelings of self-worth with fleeting highs such as money or the number of socks you have in your drawer. However, it should NEVER be considered to liken who you are as a person to ANYTHING remotely resembling anything.

There is no such thing as being a prick to get a service because of who you are, or from whom you were sired from or what you have done in your life. You still breathe the same air and drink water, just like the rest of people do.

Jealousy comes in the case where a young man who thought his relationship with his significant other would end in marriage, but it abruptly ended. This would lead to a case of lost identity, as he would now wonder what to do with himself. In the case where a person used to wearing the trending fashionable footwear and finds themselves in a position where they cannot afford to buy the expensive shoes anymore would find themselves in agony wondering what happened to their life.

This fixing of labels on our daily lives affects us in every way it can, even when we have no idea it is. It is almost as if one is in critical condition in the ICU and is closer to dying than breakfast roadkill. The level of ego one has to be in order to get this far is unfathomable, and a passionate retaliation to losing yourself to material lifestyles is commonly heard of and experienced.

How to deal with this level of egoistic tendencies:

Several quotes and books have been spoken and written to signify the bond of searching for your true soul. Climb that mountain. Take that road trip alone or with your dog. Adopt a dog. Learn a new style to cooking or fixing your roof. Ensure that the jealousy that could come up because of fear of losing yourself to material things comes to pass and never catches up with you ever again.

Here is the thing to hold dear in the hard times when you need a word of wisdom and your mind can't come up with cool Gandhi quotes; the person who you portray to the outside world is not you. The title you have at work is not the real you. The role you have in your organization is not you. The person you portray at home is not you. The person you act out to be is not you. The pain and suffering and joy and sorrow that happen to you are not you either. Only the spark, the consciousness that is inside of you is you.

c.) Low self-esteem

Solemn and glum souls reflect on the outside. Sometimes the people with this dark cloud hovering above them feel undeserving of the good things that life has to offer and may be more in fear of losing whatever good thing they have left than the next guy. In this situation, you might find the great guy with unfortunate self-esteem issues, who has the really cute girl may be inclined to be overly protective and jealous of even the coffee man.

The same can apply to friendships, with people becoming overprotective, jealous, and controlling in an attempt to keep their friends from abandoning them.

Neediness makes people with low self-esteem hold on more tightly to the things they have, and react with jealousy if they perceive a risk of it being taken away from them.

The things that make people have issues of low self-esteem are covered in chapter three of this book, but in the spirit of clarification and being thorough, one of the leading factors is a loose relationship with the caregivers who could be parents or guardians or older siblings, or seeing friends achieve something you wished to achieve but could not, like getting into a serious relationship that could potentially lead to marriage.

Constantly finding yourself to be a judgmental person can make it increasingly difficult to sustain relationships for a long time. It can even make it achingly painful to see someone who you thought of and called out as a failure succeeding in life, while there you are, stuck in the same place for years on end. Low self-esteem can result from this if not nipped in the bud early enough.

Reminding yourself each time you wake up along with the daily morning mantras that no one is ever above or below you, regardless of what they have accomplished in life, will help you see life in a deeper perspective and to always have something to look forward to.

It is important to you, dear reader, that you know that your lack of 'success' has nothing to do with your personality. Success is in quotes to put into context that the definition of the word is dependent upon the person using it. And to be quite honest, success is overrated anyway. The works of achievements that others have accomplished have nothing on you either. Just be strong as you are and fight the good fight.

Low self-esteem issues coupled with the narcissistic tendency to place achievements first and use them as a means to feel great about yourself may mean it's time to change your tire. Jealousy will creep up on you really soon.

d.) Belief that anger and spite will get you the results you want

Ever since anyone can remember their memories as a child, bad habits were rewarded with negative comments from our parents and/or guardians. It came sometimes with a bit of hiding (thanks mom and dad, for most of us wouldn't be here without you).

In lieu of this, we accepted our mistakes and took full responsibility for our actions (not entirely, but there was no other choice. Oliver Twist was just a fairy tale and the streets were harder). It only, therefore, made sense then that if you're angry (a common ingredient of jealousy), you always get what you want. Even if we don't acknowledge this belief consciously, there may be a part of us that believes that if we react to a situation with angry jealousy, somehow it will succeed in getting us what we want.

3. Jealousy and spiritualism. Are they linked?

a.) The mentality that there are differences in being among different people.

There is a theme in the America that we are all indoctrinated to believe, that we are all entities floating in the winds of the universe waiting for divine intervention to lead us along the path of righteousness. Children are encouraged when still young to be unique and to always be the first and win.

Due to this case of 'individualism', we tend to believe some of us are not worthy of the rights and privileges we enjoy. This deprives us of the joy of oneness, breeding hate and jealousy because of the thought that we deserve better than others. This is a tendency often seen in political rallies where one candidate beats the others down by saying how better he or she is.

Achieving oneness through thinking like a hive mind.

A hive mind can be related to how bees live and coexist with one another. They follow a certain sense of hierarchy and respect the rules of the system. They all have one collective agenda- to serve their queen. Spiritualism offers a conviction that we as humans are part of a hive mind. Rather than be as we are today, entangled in individualism and conceit, it explains that there is a thread connecting all of us into one unit. Think of it like the Musketeers from old France with their creed. Seeing the world through this eye glass can open you up to a world of endless possibilities. Your friend's success ultimately becomes your own success, and you will strive to help them achieve it, and in your own way be successful too.

This, in reality, takes jealousy out of the equation.

b.) Tricking the mind into hunger.

What this entails is tricking the mind into believing that there is a lack of resources out there and that only you were meant to go out and take it all for personal gain and use. Resentment can clearly come off of this, as well as jealousy, and this can be found quite frankly in over ambitious people.

Dealing with this appropriately:

Luckily, this is a mentality that can be tweaked and put into our control. It is a choice, you see, a choice to see the world as an abundance of infinite resources with enough to go around for everyone. When your neighbor is passed on to get a good fortune, then your chance of being in luck as he or she is still the same, and it is only for you to go out there and find it.

Spiritually speaking, if you really look for something and truly want it badly, the universe shall give it unto you. It is the universal law of Ask and It shall be given unto you. It does not only work in the old biblical days.

Try it and see some great things happen in your life.

c.) Law of attraction gone wrong.

In some cases, some people find themselves attracting the wrong mentalities and focusing on the wrong ideologies that may make them get jealous in turn. This is because they focus on getting their fears more than what would bring them happiness.

Positivity is the only way to counter bad vibes. Think and breathe like a child and you shall never be disappointed.

Chapter 5: Triggers of Jealousy

A breach of trust and several other qualities as will be discussed below leads to the creeping in of jealousy. Trust goes both ways; to others and to oneself. Let's look into some of the triggers of jealousy in detail;

The fear of being replaced

Being threatened by certain situations breeds jealousy. A form of jealousy is sibling jealousy that is caused by the irrational fear that their parents will love any one of their other siblings more than them. Most commonly seen in romantic affairs, jealousy is triggered by a third person, who does not necessarily impose a threat, but their mere presence is enough to bring in the green-eyed monster.

Those who live in fear are afraid to lose what they hold most dear to themselves as they, unfortunately, do not think they have what it takes to get it back or something better. This, in turn, makes them clingy and possessive, and quite possibly, dangerous.

Individual mentality

Individuality is as spontaneous as cow glue. Prior experiences of relationships gone wrong increase the likelihood of particular individual cases getting jealous. When a person has gone through a tough heartbreak more than once in a relationship prior to the current one, it will be quite difficult for them to go all out and love or trust someone like that ever again. It might be that they might commit to a relationship, but they will never let their guard down and accept to be hurt like that in the future. Case example being a person who was cheated on before; they will not let go of suspicion easily. Traits such as apprehension can also affect jealousy. People who tend to worry a lot are more likely to worry about losing a loved one.

The quality of the relationship

The occurrence of an explosive case of jealousy may arise when one is in doubt of the love a loved one gives them. It is a choice to love someone in a way that makes the relationship never lose its gusto; it is even better if the parties involved in the relationship wholeheartedly agreed to try their best to make it work. In the case of an unstable relationship, such as where the long distance calls become more and colder, the volatility may start to take shape. Volatile relationships tend to bring about this in many individuals making them highly prone to jealousy. Indeed, since jealousy is the fear of losing someone to another person, it may become unhealthy in the long term. For those relationships which are already a sinking ship, it is more important to note that jealousy may be the last hole to take it to the heart of Davy Jones' Locker. How two or more people relate in a relationship speaks volumes of how and when the jealousy may find its way into their connection.

Chapter 6: The 7 Ladders to Smoothly Overcome Jealousy in a Relationship

Smoothly overcoming jealousy may seem like an impossible task due to hurt feelings and painful backlash of words between partners, but it can be achieved through patience, perseverance and sticking to the following few steps:

1) This might sound a little cliché, but how about you believe your partner once in a while?

Surely this must be wrong, you might think, but why not take their word for it? Remember that if they do lie to you in your face, then they are only making a fool out of themselves. Trust is the foundation of every relationship, and it would be quite insulting of you to your significant other if you always give a shred of doubt with them at all times. Frequent buggering can be quite destructive as cheating in the long term.

Of course, you will still not trust your significant other for a while out of common routine, but the vigor to act as if you do believe them will rise from within. When they say they love you, believe them, and stop checking in at all times if they're where they say they are or with whom. Try your best to pretend to believe them, and with time they will see the sense of being honest with you. Eventually, the lies will stop, and a seamless sailing will occur.

2) Hark the wisdom knocks and says unto thee; quit comparing yourself to others.

Not all jealousy is driven by low self-esteem, but some are. None of us is ever going to comprehend why another person loves us. It's like arguing out if Siri, Apple's Artificial Intelligence for iPhones, knows what diverse implications it could cause if someone was to ask why their milk is frothy when boiled. Consider this my friend; that there are much better people than just about any one of us out there, but your significant other chose you because of that underlying spark inside you that they could not find anywhere else or with anyone else. The most notable people in history are way low on the list of looks or wealth, so stop worrying about working out why they could ever want to be with you.

3) It is wise to always prepare for everything, including preparing yourself to lose them.

It is not the best idea or thought to have, but it is a wise one. Not all jealousy is experienced by people with low esteem, for even those with high self-esteem are ranked to have the most intense levels of jealousy. This is so because they always have a tendency of being the center of the universe. Such flavors of people tend to have a view of people as material possessions, and quite right have the contentment to "share " their "property", not for a smile or a look at any other person at all. It is highly likely that they were spoiled brats as children.

It is a point to cautiously note that people are not playthings or toys to be constantly protected. To love someone or something you must be willing and ready to let them go at whatever the cost. Once you have accepted the fact that your actions might be the cause for the abrupt end of your relationship, it would be a good strategy to air it out with your partner. If all else fails, amicably agree to let bygones be bygones and part your ways in a friendly way.

Really, is this so? You ask, but wait, there's more to justify these claims;

Overprotective nature, anger, and jealousy drive love away fast, and love needs courage and bravery as spices to prosper. There is the natural fear of losing someone you hold dear to you, and obviously how that will make you feel. When imagination comes to play in this case, stretch that glorious mind into working out a scenario where the worst has happened and you are still alright. Not just alright, but flourishing in that imagined scenario.

Visualize about how well you would react in that situation, and keep playing back that Kelly Clarkson jam in your mind,"What doesn't kill you makes you stronger"

A hush point to note...keep this list in your memory palace, and not anywhere your significant other can find it. We don't want them feeling insecure, now do we?

4) Never consider even fathoming to play games. It's that serious.

We all know how uncomfortable jealousy makes the average person. It is unfortunate that people try to make themselves feel better by making their significant others jealous of them. Whoever coined the term 'Two can play that game' was holistically wrong on the matter. Never do this. All it does is lower the respect your partner has for you and degrades the love they have for you in the long term.

It is quite alright to have a look at that eye candy going down the block, but never use it as firepower to attack your partner. They say that if someone calls you names it should never hurt you; even if it does, you can take the comfort of knowing that their words reflect themselves and are not in any way a

5) Quit replacing reality with building castles in the sky.

Imagination is a powerful tool that creates scenes of your significant other cheating on you and propounds jealousy in huge doses. We as humans are so much bigger on the inside and can never get bored at all if we allow the exploration of the imagination station. If I sit back and imagine myself having a drink with Johnny Depp and spaceship lands on the patio and an alien with a burrito for a hand stumbles out, I have the pleasure of imagining it and doing whatever I want with that line of that, but it doesn't mean that I believe it.

Say for example, your partner is home later than you thought they were going to be, the moment you take the steps not to become emotional with imagined scenarios of your significant other cheating on you, that is the moment you have taken a bold step into overcoming jealousy.

6) Give them a little more rope.

Not to hang themselves (Jeez no!), or make a lasso with it (though this would be cool on another scale), but some space. Give your partner space. If your significant other wants to visit their friends from way back in college or long lost friends from back home, let them. They are their own individuals and have the right to do as they please. If you do not let them lead their own lives they will feel like hostages and will want to escape from that life you are giving them. Let them be free as they should, but this is not an excuse to let them walk over you. If you find yourself suspecting your significant other of trying to make you jealous, curb this by being chill about it, and be the better person and nip it in the bud. Talk to them, and before that, make it as spicy as you can. The situation could be used to your advantage and rekindle the flame of passion.

How? You may ask...by following step number 7.

7) Making beautiful use of that imagination to make you feel better, and not uncomfortably worse.

Chapter 7: 7 Steps to Deal with Jealousy

Since seven is the lucky go-to number when gambling or finding the best playlist on a road trip or praying for a great week, here is a list of 7 phases or stages, if you will, to deal with jealousy. It is wise to note your bravery for being at this stage of discovery. From the following scenarios, you understand you have the feeling of jealousy with your partner, and now want to be better than your emotions.

1. Take a wise step back and evaluate your relationship.

Arguably one of the best ways to overcome jealousy is to first and foremost take a step back and assess your relationship. What this implies is to purposefully reflect on the foundation of your relationship, and consider if your partner's behavior reflects upon these values, be it trust, intimacy, commitment, or communication. A breather is always considered the healthiest way to come to terms with reality and grasp the implications of actions to be taken in the future.

If you feel they are not truly being honest with you, this can trigger a bout of insecurities. This is where it might get ugly. A lack of communication with your partner will always lead to this. Most fathers and sons rarely bond because of this, accrediting it to being manly and not talking about what they feel until it's too late for the relationship. A wise decision would be to come to terms with the fact that time moves regardless of good tidings or terrible moments, and it would be best to make the most of it.

When you find yourself in an insecure relationship, you should always expect your buttons to be pushed when it comes to jealousy. There is no one who can advise you on what to do but you. Staying will definitely leave you feeling terrible and very jealous almost all the time.

2. Take a breather and self-assess.

When you find yourself feeling insecure and untrusting in a relationship that has a solid foundation and is built on trust and honesty, you really need to take a glass of cold water, find a nice tree, like one that jumped right out of a Robert Frost poem, and sit under it with a good book and a picnic blanket to reevaluate your purpose in that relationship. It might be necessary to take a day off for this.

Perhaps you might find yourself to be a little too attached than usual, and this could be the reason to have such inclinations of jealous responses. Don't you worry; you are not alone in this.

There are those who have developed safe and secure attachments with their loved ones along their early years, and these are the ones who are inclined to be less jealous and clingy, have glowing social tendencies and high self-esteem, coupled with fewer feelings of inadequacy.

It is imperative to ask yourself these questions when it comes to that point of self-discovery:

Does your soul feel empty and filled with a void?

How were previous relationships with loved ones?

How was the environment back at home? Warm? Loving? Heated?

Was your upbringing a harsh one filled with repression?

When you were a child were your guardians undependable?

The levels of attachment vary from person to person, and much later in life experiences and circumstances influence that level.

3. Always ask for help.

You're not being weak by doing so. You have friends, church help group, your local garbage man, or you can even find a random stranger. Talk to them. Problems half shared are problems half solved. Talk to someone other than your partner if you need a second opinion, but always consider talking about your feelings to your partner.

4. Accept that you are jealous.

Acceptance is the door to a happier life. Admitting that you are jealous opens a door to learning, and healing. Think of it like church, or anyone who has any seed of faith- naming the evil makes it lose its potency since one is no longer letting it humiliate them.

5. Lick your wounds and learn from that misstep.

Jealousy is an opportunity to go higher and move stronger. The moment you realize your friend writes excellent programs and creates amazing websites, instead of wallowing in jealousy and self-pity, you sign up for coding and graphic design classes.

6. Let the pain go and manage your feelings in a healthy manner.

In the words of the Doctor (no relation, only wishful thinking...), take all that pain and negativity and jealousy in your hand and put a fist around it, and say - never again. Breathe in and tell yourself you don't need that kind of bad vibe flowing through you. Let it go like a fart in the wind, never to be seen again. The best part is you can repeat it as many times as you want. Fun, isn't it?

Calmness is letting words and insults and emotions wash over you like water over stone. Taking in several breaths at a time help one detach from intense emotions. It is necessary to share feelings of deep jealousy after you calm down.

Sometimes all one needs is to get their gears rolling. Take a jog or a walk or write it down in a journal.

7. Always keep a reminder of your good side.

We all have a yin and yang, a good side and bad side and strength and weaknesses. Again, jealousy is a normal reaction. It becomes difficult to deal with when it becomes constant.

A point to note is to try your best to avoid alcohol or illegal drugs, as well as caffeine when experiencing stressful emotions. They tend to exaggerate mood swings and increase the chances of acting inappropriately.

Conclusion

In summary, as all good things come to an end, it is quite classical to review what the matter at hand is, and its drastic effects on life as an unchecked emotion. From the early days of mythology to the current century, jealousy still haunts our very being and meaning as a human race. The autonomy of belief in the thread that connects us all is quite strong in religious and spiritual grounds.

Jealousy is a disease, as well as a cure. This can be quite ironic, coming from the source of all good things reputable. Clearly, the human race needs to work on the relationship standards, before we can say we are fully developing into a universal oneness.

We have delved deep into the emotion that spells fear, doubt, clouds judgment, and destroys relationships. We have also seen how the wise can use this emotion to get ahead in building their relationships, breed trust, and enhance friendships and familial bonds with their siblings and parents.

Therefore the next time you get the chance with your significant other to play the jealous victim role, always put yourself in their shoes and mull over some few thoughts;

Are these feelings new?

Could it not be the first time they're acting this way?

It is imperative to note that someone with a tendency and nature to be obsessive and controlling even in their previous relationships will not go down easy. Time and a lot of it will be spent in much-needed therapy sessions with a professional.

You will be lucky to find a partner willing to change and take the steps necessary to take control of their emotions.

It would be wise to say that using everything at hand, including emotions as a tool to make things better in our daily lives, is a skill learned and should be used at every opportunity when necessary.

Chances to be overwhelmed with jealousy should be overcome by taking heed to the steps outlined in this book, as well as taking the chance to repair the cracks in any relationship. The beginning and end of a relationship is a choice. One chooses to love another, and should, therefore, be prepared to take on any hurdle to come their way, including painful moments of emotion, and learn to use that obstacle to build something better than it was before.

Anger Management

7 Steps to Freedom from Anger, Stress, and Anxiety

Introduction:
The Anger Problem

Congratulations on purchasing your personal copy of *Anger Management: 7 Steps to Freedom from Anger, Stress, and Anxiety*. Thank you for doing so.

Everyone knows how anger feels since we have all experienced it, whether just as a momentary annoyance or full-on rage-filled fury. Anger is normal and usually healthy for those who experience it. However, when this normal emotion is allowed to run rampant and turn destructive, it causes many issues with personal relationships, your career, and eventually poisons your entire life. In addition, anger can lead you to feel like you're being controlled by something powerful and unpredictable. This book is intended to help you both control and understand anger.

The Norm of Anger and Attack Tactics:

Perhaps it's a bit ironic that during this modern age of positive thinking and psychology, anger is one of the most commonly expressed emotions on a social level. Countless politicians have thrown in the towel on trying to give a dignified debate. Instead, they scream, yell, shove, and push at the slightest provocation. There was a time when attack advertisements were only reserved for very serious or bad situations, but this is now the most common tactic used in politics.

These attacks aren't only reserved for political views and even go into personal details about the politician's life. These attacks may occur in comments that are meant to be off the record or show up in voice recordings.

But this anger is not limited to just politics. It seems like a daily occurrence that we either read about or witness someone attacking a customer service agent, drivers and their road rage and outbursts of overworked professionals. There are plenty of theories about where this comes from, ranging from a lack of home stability, the state of the economy, teachers failing to instill politeness in their pupils, the Internet, the government, or even food chemicals.

Reasons behind the Anger Problem:

Brain and Psychology researchers discuss the amygdala (which controls our emotions in the brain) being too small or too large, or even underdeveloped pre-frontal cortexes in the brain (which are responsible for planning). Social studies look to the role of vicarious reinforcement and modeling for triggering this angry, aggressive behavior, while other psychologists blame this aggression on weak superegos. The bottom line is that there are theories everywhere, but the problem persists.

The following chapters will discuss some of the many ways you can better understand the issue of anger in yourself (and the anger of others), so you can fix the problem and stop letting this aggression run your life.

There are plenty of books on this subject on the market, thanks again for choosing this one! Every effort was made to ensure it is full of as much useful information as possible. Please enjoy!

Chapter 1: The Origins of Anger

Anger is a state of emotion that spans from light irritation to overwhelming rage and fury. Similar to other feelings, anger is accompanied by biological and physiological changes. As soon as you get angry, your blood pressure and heart rate increase along with the energy hormones noradrenaline and adrenaline. Anger is caused by internal and external events alike.

You might get angry at someone, like a supervisor or coworker, or a situation (such as a canceled flight or traffic jam), or you might get angry from brooding or worrying about personal issues in your life. In addition, remembering enraging or traumatic events can trigger this emotion. Where exactly does this problematic tendency come from? Understanding this will help you get your own anger and frustration under control so that you can lead a free and healthy life.

The Increasingly Angry World:

We gave some possible explanations for the norm of anger in the introduction to this book. Even professional psychologists who study anger don't have all the answers, but social factors play a large role. Apart from physical brain factors, the social order does seem to be coming unglued in a few different ways, including the polarization of the political spectrum, the shrinking economy, and reality TV. But there are some subtle, smaller ways that we are losing our composure.

Depictions of Anger on Television:

Anger is slowly becoming the norm. First instance, consider the way some television shows depict characters consulting professionals for advice on something, such as lawyers, nurses, or doctors. If someone on House, for instance, doesn't approve of his diagnosis, he will curse at his doctor. In everyday shows that many people watch, the characters speak to each other as though they are enemies, and this is considered normal.

The Role of Observing Aggression:

Observing this aggressive behavior, especially when it doesn't cause negative results, could be playing an important role in provoking aggressive outbursts in the average person. Human behavior studies involve a lot of factors that might compound upon each other, which explains why the area often uses nonhuman animals to get its results. One study done recently by Loyola University tested the idea that passive observation and brain chemistry can lead to higher aggressive actions in mice.

The mice who observed angry behavior in other mice developed a higher amount of neural receptivity in their brains than the mice who didn't. In other words, by just watching their rodent companions fight, the ones observing developed a higher tendency toward feeling aggression in themselves.

Childhood Aggression and Modeling:

Ironically, the increasingly violent cartoons of the '50s are what led psychologists to look into modeling's role in aggression in kids. The idea that the more kids watched violent shows, the more they showed violent tendencies, supported the conclusion that anger breeds anger.

This is one of the many reasons why the study about the mice above is so valuable. You might wonder, then, where the anger originally came from.

Presumably, anger and aggression have always existed in humans. A world free from violence will probably never exist, but the problem is determining its consequences. This behavior will never stop if no obvious consequences occur, escalating and eventually causing more harm.

Too much Violence and Rage?

If the consensus is that too much violence, rage, and aggression is being perpetuated in society and the media, what are we to do? The tide is probably too advanced to stop completely, but we can hope that manners will become popular again. In the meantime, it's up to the individual to notice when they are acting inappropriate and learn to control their own aggression. You can start by taking responsibility for the role you play yourself in this societal problem.

The Expression of Anger:

The natural, instinctive way to express a feeling of anger is to act in an aggressive way. Anger is an adaptive, natural reaction to a threat and inspires strong, usually aggressive behaviors and feelings in us. This allows us to defend ourselves and fight when we are under threat or attack. A certain level of this emotion, then, is needed for our species to survive.

But we cannot reasonably lash out physically every time someone or something annoys or irritates us. Common sense, social norms, laws, and our own sanity put limits onto how much we can express this emotion. Plus, it wouldn't be good for us to act on every impulse we have that comes from anger. Society could never have progressed if everyone did this. There's a reason we matured past this.

The Three Approaches to Anger:

Most individuals use a variety of unconscious and conscious methods for dealing with anger, which is calming, suppressing, and expressing. Let's look closer at each of these ways of dealing with it.

- **Expression:** Expressing anger in a way that is assertive instead of aggressive is the healthiest method of dealing with anger. In order to do this right, you must find out how to express your needs and meet them without harming other people. Assertiveness does not translate to being demanding or pushy with others, but being respectful both to others and yourself.

- **Suppression**: Alternatively, you can suppress anger, then redirect or convert it later on. This process occurs when you keep your anger inside, make yourself stop focusing on it, then redirect your mind to something more positive. The goal here is to suppress and inhibit the angry feeling, converting it to something more constructive and positive. The problem with this reaction is that if your anger isn't expressed outwardly, it can turn toward yourself. Inward anger may lead to depression, high blood pressure, hypertension, and other issues.

  Suppressing anger can lead to other issues for you, including pathological anger expressions, including passive aggression, or a hostile and cynical personality. Individuals who put other people down constantly, are always critical and make cynical comments are a perfect example of the consequences of not learning how to express anger constructively. People like this are, not surprisingly, not very likely to enjoy success with their relationships.

- **Calming Down**: The last method for dealing with anger is calming down inside. What this means is not only controlling the way you act outwardly, but controlling the responses you have inside, actively lowering your pulse, allowing the emotions to pass, and intentionally calming yourself.

The Anger Management Goal:

The main goal of learning about anger management should be reducing the physiological response and emotional feelings of anger. You can not avoid or get rid of the people or things that cause you to get mad, and you can't change most of them. Your reactions, however, are always within your control.

How can you Know if you're too Angry?

Now that you know the harm anger can cause, how are you to know if you need to work on your own anger? There are some tests out there that can gauge the intensity of this emotion, along with your abilities to handle it and how prone you are to anger. But the odds are high that if you have an anger issue, you're already well aware of it. After all, you're reading this book! If you notice that you act in frightening or out of control ways, you may need assistance in dealing with your anger.

What makes some Individuals Angrier than Other Individuals?

According to experts, certain people just have hotter heads than other people, getting mad faster and more intensely than is most common. There are also plenty of people who aren't as outwardly expressive with their angry feelings but who are always grumpy and irritable. People who are easily angered do not always throw things or curse, at times they just get ill, sulk, or withdraw socially.

People who get mad easily usually have what is known as a low frustration tolerance. In other words, they feel like they don't deserve to feel annoyance, inconvenience, or frustration in life. These people don't know how to take the events of life in stride and get especially mad when they encounter an "unfair" situation, such as being corrected.

The Causes of Easy Frustration:

What is that makes someone more prone to easy frustration? There are numerous factors at play here.

- **Genetics or Physiology:** One cause could be physiological properties or genetics. In fact, evidence exists that some kids are just born easily angered, touchy, or irritable and show these signals from a very young age.
- **Sociocultural Factors:** Another possible cause for getting easily angered is sociocultural factors. Anger is usually seen as something negative. Most of us are taught that we can show sadness or anxiety, but that anger is not tolerable. This can lead to an inability to channel the feeling in a constructive manner.

- **Family Background:** Studies have shown that family life also plays a big role in anger. Usually, those who get mad easily come from a background full of angry family members or a chaotic, disruptive home life. If a child is never taught how to deal with their anger, they likely won't be very good at communicating their emotions in a healthy way.

Should you Openly Express your Anger?

Some believe and claim that letting your anger show is the best way to prevent the harmful impacts of suppressing or ignoring it. Is this a good idea?

Professional psychologists are now stating that this is not a good idea. Some individuals will use the theory above as an excuse to be hurtful to those around them. Studies have shown that just letting your anger flow uninhibited actually causes aggression to escalate and doesn't help you fix the situation at all. The best approach is to figure out what is causing your anger and then to come up with methods for keeping these triggers in check instead of letting them send you flying off the handle.

Chapter 2: What is Anger good for?

Emotions are there for a reason, but anger can often seem pointless, confusing, or even harmful. Anytime you aren't getting what you wish for, or you get something you fear; it may cause anger to appear. Be careful, because excessive anger can cause divorce, damage your children, and harm your relationships at work and home. How effective are you at controlling your anger? In order to help prevent this from becoming a problem, learn to see this emotion as a sign that you should pause.

Anger, The Chemical Response:

Anger is triggered in reaction to chemicals from your primitive lower and middle brain areas. These chemicals are meant to mobilize us for defensive action to prevent harm. These chemicals are sending the message "GO!" to our body, spurring the animal to get what it needs to survive, by force if necessary. This helped us evolve by getting food first, dominating an enemy, or scaring off predators. It mobilizes your body for action to achieve important goals.

Anger to Self Soothe Neuro-chemically:

With some exceptions that are few and far between, most angry people have a problem with their self-image or self-esteem. A lot of them have success with their jobs but have a hard time with relationships, where there are plenty of anger triggers. Apart from their professional success, though, nearly all of these people have thoughts that they aren't good enough.

There is actually a chemical explanation for how the emotion of anger (at least temporarily) can be a type of soothing mechanism psychologically. The brain releases a hormone called norepinephrine when anger is sparked, which the brain experiences as an analgesic.

The Numbing Effect:

Whether someone is confronted with psychological or physical pain (or even the fear of pain like this), the response of anger helps to release chemicals to numb it. So anger is not a pointless emotion and exists for a reason. Anger can harm relationships, sure, but it's also important for helping vulnerable individuals survive relationships and life, in general.

Covering Core Pain:

This kind of anger is there to mask the core pains we all have. The key, stressful feelings that are within these core pains are feeling unloved, powerless, rejected, guilty, accused, unimportant, or ignored. All of these build an identity that is based on shame. It's only reasonable, then, that if eliciting anger in yourself can help to mask these unbearable or hurtful feelings, a person could eventually grow dependent on these feelings until they are addicted to them.

The idea of soothing oneself is very relevant in this regard. Everyone has to find ways to reassure or comfort themselves when his or her sense of identity is under threat, rather through dismissal, criticism, or some other outside event that leads the to feel invalidated or doubt themselves. If someone is healthy on a psychological level, he or she can use his or her inner resources to validate themselves, to admit that he or she might have made a mistake without suffering intolerable shame or guilt. However, if they don't feel good about themselves deep down, their sense of self will be unable to withstand these threats.

Anger as the Remedy:

What is the remedy for this situation? Even though it seems paradoxical, anger can be a way to soothe yourself, even though the emotion can destroy wellbeing and peace of mind. This is because our anger can invalidate whatever or whoever caused us to suffer a feeling of invalidation. If we adamantly deny the threat outside of us, we can claim that our own point of view is superior, restoring our mental and emotional security. Although our state of mind is not in harmony, and we might actually feel bad inside, our anger is still a defense that lets us feel more comfortable than we did before.

Invalidating Others:

This helps us think that we are not the ones that are inconsiderate, selfish, bad, or in the wrong. It must be our co-worker, neighbor, our child, or our partner. True, our desperate response might be a way to self-soothe as the last possible resort, but it does work as a self-soothing mechanism, nonetheless. Simply put, if you cannot offer yourself comfort through validating yourself, this will be done by the invalidation of other people. And those who have severe depression usually haven't figured out how to get rid of this powerful but self-destructive defense mechanism.

Anger for Self-Empowerment:

Since anger helps us to medicate ourselves against pain on a psychological level, it's also effective for warding off powerlessness or other doubtful feelings. Our brain releases the numbing feeling when we get provoked, but it also releases amphetamine-related hormones, which allow us to feel energized by adrenaline. This can seem adaptive and very tempting. If a situation or person leads us to feel powerless or defeated, we can reactively transform those uncomfortable emotions into righteous anger and feel in control again.

The Cost of Lacking Skills in Anger Management:

But when someone doesn't have skills for managing his or her anger, instead of exploding aggressively, their reactions are very likely to lead to serious problems. These outbursts might get them what they want at the moment, but it clashes with other important needs. People wish to be loved and liked. Although anger may get you what you want in the immediate moment, it will weaken your attractiveness in terms of family connections, friendships, and work situations. To put it simply, angry people are less liked than agreeable people.

Anger helps you Notice Problems:

As soon as anger has shown you that you need to pay attention, it's done its job. But the madder you get, the less likely you are to effectively solve the issue. This is because aggression decreases your thinking ability, your ability to notice new information, to form new perspectives, or to create a good solution. Similar to your laptop, overheating will freeze up your data-processing mechanisms, shutting you down. As soon as anger has shown you that you need to pause because there's a problem, the best course of action is to obey this instruction.

Remembering to Pause:

The trick to controlling your anger is to keep in mind that it's meant to remind you to pause what you're doing. Anger shows you that you need to pause, listen, and look at your surroundings. Stop proceeding with the situation, stop and remind yourself to first lower your feelings of rage and aggression. Do some deep breathing, distract your mind with something more positive, relax your muscles, count backwards from 100, do whatever works best for you to pause.

Change the Subject:

Changing the subject can aid you in pausing a heated conversation or interaction, pausing the anger effectively. You can make a pleasant comment that derails the path that you were on previously. If this doesn't work for calming down the anger inside you, simply excuse yourself. You can say that you need to step outside or get some water.

This is your chance to soothe yourself using methods such as reading something, slowing your breath, or looking at pictures of cute puppies online. As soon as you've returned to calmness, you may start planning out the method you'll use to handle whatever situation is troubling you. Think of this as a time-out you give to yourself, as a parent gives to their toddler in the throes of a temper tantrum.

Pay Attention:

The next step here is to pay attention to the situation, seeing it from a different point of view that helps you figure out what you truly need and want from it. Come up with a smarter way to communicate than just attacking your conversation partner with words until you achieve your goals. Keep in mind that you may use words in a constructive way to think about the situation, come up with a plan, and address your concerns. You can use your logical reasoning abilities, as a human, to plan out what you can do differently the next time around.

Be Careful:

Be careful and steer clear of the trap that is always present when considering a difficult, anger-inducing problem or situation. Remember that you should be focusing on yourself instead of the event or person you're mad at. Stay away from thoughts about how you want the situation or person to change to make you happy. Thinking about how the person made you mad or what they should do to make up for what they did will only feed your anger and frustration.

Focus on you:

You should focus on what you can do to fix what happened, and on how you can change to be better at handling problems in the future. Becoming empowered to make changes yourself instead of thinking about controlling the other person or the situation is one key way to calmly handle anger with poise.

This will also help you overcome the urge to handle difficult scenarios with anger and aggression. Remind yourself repeatedly, starting from when the anger first starts appearing within you, that your job is to find what you can do to change the situation, not to control others.

Practice Listening:

This part is perhaps the most challenging of all. At this stage, you need to ask the other about their concerns. Make yourself stay calm and refrain from reacting, as you listen to them and search for the common ground between you two. Listen to them to gain a true understanding of what they feel, rather than defensively responding or attacking their point of view, as you may wish to do at the moment. Actually, the madder you are, the harder it will be to truly listen to the other person.

This is because when anger is present, it makes you feel like your desires are sacred and that others' don't matter. Your wishes will appear gigantic, as the other person's wishes shrink down to nothing.

Be Fully Calm:

This is why you must make sure you've calmed yourself all the way when you first pause. This is essential for true listening and will allow you to rise to the challenge of understanding the concerns of the other person. Thankfully, if you do truly listen fully enough to understand their perspective, you're going to have better odds of reaching your own goals, too. Even if this sounds paradoxical, it's the truth, as all skilled salespeople already know. The more in tune a salesperson is when their client's concerns, the better chance they have at reaching the agreement they want in the end. Remember that in order to reliably control your anger, when you get mad, pause.

Relationships, Health, and Self-Esteem:

The majority of people know that there's a connection between persistent anger and physical issues, such as heart disease. But anger also has other more obvious, immediate effects on the sufferer. It uses up a lot of physical and mental energy, steals your enjoyment of life, gets in the way of useful and constructive thinking, and harms your career and relationship prospects. Anger can also hurt your self-esteem and cause you to obsess over the negative thoughts circling in your mind.

Anger Victimizes you:

Once you have an aggressive exchange, you will suffer the effects for a while after, as you repeat what happened over and over in your head, bringing up the angry emotions again and adding power to them repeatedly. During this time, your emotions will be controlled by these angry memories, causing you to be victimized by your feelings.

Anytime you let someone's actions cause you anger, you're being victimized by your feelings. That person has probably already forgotten about the event while you are controlled by it. As you fret and fume and go over the event repeatedly, you are missing out on spending time with your family, relaxing on your day off, or while trying to fall asleep in your bed at home. As you can see, learning how to get this under control is very important for a happy, fulfilled life.

Chapter 3: Justified vs. Unjustified Anger

Plenty of Americans go around feeling angry these days, and some have more justified reasons for this than others. Let's look at the differences between unjustified and justified anger.

Justified Anger:

People who are justified in their anger are the homeless, the unemployed, those who are hungry or who are taking on unmanageable tax burdens. Someone who cannot afford an education has justified anger or those who don't have enough health care. Those who have lost loved ones to war or who don't feel as though they have a choice in political situations all have justified anger, as well.

Unjustified Anger:

The people who have unjustified anger include people who don't take responsibility for their own actions, who blame others, or who feel as though they are always being victimized by life circumstances. It's the ones who always put their own needs first and don't think about others.

Does Anger give you the Illusion of Control?

If anger makes you feel as though you're actually in control, you will have a hard time controlling your anger. This heading sums up a lot of people's problem with anger. For those who are interested in this emotion, it can be hard to find clinical literature on it. But this is starting to change. With drive-by shootings, road rage, and high school killing sprees on the rise, people are starting to play closer attention to acting out, extreme anger, and acts of aggression.

Suddenly, paying attention to warning signs of anger seems a lot more important. Within the last 15 years, at least 50 books have emerged on the subject of anger. In the year 1995, a professional book called *Anger Disorders: Definition, Diagnosis, and Treatment* came out that proposed some diagnostic categories to handle anger as a syndrome, instead of a feeling connected to different disorders.

The following will be an attempt to make sense of the anger-related, self-defeating actions that arise from this emotion.

The Forgotten Defense:

Anger can be thought of as the forgotten defense of Freud. If, in Freud's opinion, every defense mechanism of the human mind is there to protect our personalities from the anxiety that comes from the ego being attacked, it's weird that he didn't consider anger as part of this.

Anger as Camouflage:

But when it comes to an essential human feeling that is mainly there to protect someone from another feeling, anger might be the exception. Anger almost never exists as the main, primary emotion. Even when it appears to be a knee-jerk, instantaneous response to being provoked, there is usually another feeling that was their fist. This primary feeling is what your anger is popping up to control or attempt to camouflage.

The Road Rage Example:

A simple example of this idea of anger would be the extremely frustrating experience of someone cutting you off in traffic. Nearly everyone that experiences this event reacts with anger. However, when you look deeper at what getting cut off in traffic usually involves, the danger of getting into a life-threatening accident, they notice that at the moment before taking action to avoid the crash, they felt some kind of fear or apprehension.

Switching from this level of apprehension or fear to the intense state of anger occurs so quickly that most people can't recall the flash of fear they had felt the anger or rage took over their mind. Even rage itself appears to be a more desperate, stronger type of anger that was created in mind to get rid of the threat to one's personal safety or ego, whether this is physical, emotional, or mental.

Secondary Anger and What It Means:

The inner process happening in the above example also applies to other emotions that, one they appear, can be hidden through a flash of secondary anger. And as many psychological defenses get in the way of healthy coping mechanisms (by hiding the initial anxiety that must be faced), anger also shows how fragile the ego is that needs to be supported and shielded.

How Anger Controls us:

If anger leads us to a feeling of power and appears to be a magical solution to mask our deep fears and doubts, it's no wonder that it controls us in so many ways. In a way, anger is similar to cocaine or anger, causing strong addictions due to its illusory effect of empowering us. Though nearly no one realizes that their tendency toward getting angry is a way to cope with, intimidate, and disarm their enemy, anger is used as a way to make up for lack of self-esteem and personal power.

Unlike feeling out of control or weak, the emotion of aggression or anger causes a sensation of invincibility or invulnerability. In fact, anger can even have physical effects on someone, making them momentarily stronger with adrenaline.

Anger for Distancing in Relationships:

Anger also has a function in regulating the distance between us and others in close relationships, ensuring safety from getting hurt. If someone's parents or caretakers were untrustworthy, unreliable, or unresponsive, that person would probably grow up to be wary or defensive. They will likely cultivate a way to be emotionally detached in close relationships. Although these people might wish to form a strong bond that they've missed from childhood, they won't know how to express these desires and needs in an open, healthy way. Risking this with someone who may react in a negative way could hurt them gravely.

The Fear of Letting down your Guard:

The deep fear in these people is that letting their defense down and allowing themselves to be vulnerable, revealing their deep desire, could lead to rejection. A negative response could be very harmful to them, so they use anger as a protective measure and distance themselves as a way to survive emotionally.

Many spouses say that as soon as they notice their marriage going very well, their partner would pick a fight, probably due to feeling threatened by this closeness. Wounded psychologically from parental disregard, insensitivity, or even worse, they might have a serious distrust of getting too close to someone, defaulting to defensive anger as a way to protect themselves.

Using Anger to Push Someone Away:

On the other hand, anger can also push the other away from us, leading them to be the one to back off. If someone wants to get plenty of space and alone time, all he or she has to do is be angry all the time. This will cause others to avoid you at all costs. If we have no experience with relational intimacy, the feeling of being close to someone else can feel dangerous to our inner equilibrium, setting off alarms and causing anger. In this sense, the anger can be said to be justified, but still not healthy.

Too much Detachment:

But feeling very detached from others may also dredge up old fears and wounds, so sometimes, the one who wanted distance might pursue the other. The point to take from this is that even unconscious anger can be used in many ways that regulate the feeling of vulnerability when it comes to close relationships. This can not only be utilized to create distance with the other person when closeness causes anxiety, but can also be used as a way to try to engage the other person from a distance.

If we had an insecure or tenuous attachment to our parents growing up, it's logical that the least risky way to get attached to someone else would be using anger to create distance. Scared of being too close to someone else, but scared of completely breaking our attachment to them, getting angry easily presents a solution, even though it's unsatisfying and dysfunctional. You can ask yourself the following questions to have a better understanding of your anger:

- What skills should I learn for controlling my anger?
- What is my anger protecting me against?
- How can I address the core feeling behind my anger?

Anger can be compared to an emotion that is just the top of the iceberg. It's rarely there on its own and instead exists to hide other, deeper emotions happening below it.

Chapter 4: Handling Different Types of Anger

When something occurs that brings your anger up without warning, it can be hard not to yield to this feeling. Since you will usually get mad from feeling fearful or powerless in response to an unfair event, anger appears as your attempt to bring a fast fix to the situation. This can be compared to steeling your body against an impending attack, but it all happens on a mental level, instead of physically.

But there are many different issues that come up when you give into this push-back response of feeling angry, and the main issue is likely that the anger almost never resolves the problem that caused it to arise. This reactive feeling of anger can be best understood as a self-destructive tendency. So how can you tell how to handle your anger?

<u>Healthy, Logical Responses to Anger:</u>

For anger to be acted on in a healthy way, it has to fit into two different criteria, which is nearly impossible in every case. For your anger reaction to make sense, it must:

1. Be in response to someone who has needlessly and intentionally acted in a way that was hurtful to you, and...

2. Be advantageous or beneficial for you (as in it must help you achieve the goal you have in your mind.

I think most people will see that you can almost never claim that anger is helpful and warranted, either to you or to the situation you're dealing with at the moment. So here is an alternative to giving into anger and abandoning all reason and logic. This should neutralize your feelings of anger within just seconds, or if you're in a serious rage, in a few minutes.

How to Neutralize Rage or Anger:

Remember that, for this to work, you have to actually wish to follow these steps, have enough motivation to go through with them, and overcome the subconscious resistance that's standing in your way. Since there are some immediate benefits that come along with anger that get in the way of your determination to defeat the anger, we will go over a few advantages that could get in the way of using this method to neutralize your harmful, self-destructive feelings of anger. Here is what anger accomplishes, at least at the moment:

- **Gives you a Reward:** Anger can make you feel as though you're morally superior in the situation. That justified feeling of righteousness works temporarily to bolster a weak sense of self-esteem and is used as a defense mechanism.
- **Defends against Fear:** Anger can defend against anxiety or vulnerability. When you get that righteous rush of anger, accompanied by adrenaline, it makes you feel momentarily empowered, which is better than afraid.
- **Protects against Depression:** Anger can help you avoid feeling depression, alienation, or a deep loneliness. Even though the interaction is likely negative, anger allows you to engage with someone else.

- **(Appears to) Restore Control:** Anger can help you regain a sense of control when you get frustrated and feel as though you have none. It can temporarily put the power back into your hands, or so it seems.
- **Helps you Get what you want:** Anger can aid you in getting what you want using intimidation tactics with the other person.

The Double Step Anger Control Technique:

If you have a hard time putting the process we are going to cover below into practice, these immediate benefits to anger are likely what is causing you to have trouble. You must first realize these advantages if you are going to work through them and learn to control your anger.

Step Number 1: Relaxation.

Your first step requires that you relax. Even though anger has made you feel as though your whole body is ready to fight (inspired by adrenaline and fear), you need to find a method for discharging that energy before moving onto any action whatsoever. You must realize that in order to go into battle mode, you are activating every organ and muscle in your body automatically.

Defined in a broad way, anger is basically the reaction to a threat that you perceived, so it serves as your body's signal to get ready for combat. Since your body is mobilized for impulsive and immediate action, any reflectiveness that you use to stall would handicap this. Anger impacts your thinking as strongly as it does your physical body.

When Anger Isn't Needed:

Considering the ethnical and legal limitations of living in modern society, it's not very likely that when you get angry, you will assault your spouse or even need to defend yourself physically. But anger gets your mind ready to fight, in addition to your body, so as soon as this emotion comes over you, you've already lost your ability to assess the event objectively or logically. This makes it likely that you will attack the person verbally.

At this stage, you are not thinking from a rational, evolved point of view, but the survival-oriented, primitive, and simple brain. This simple brain can be compared to a regressed, childlike state of mind where all you can focus on is being violated, cheated, devalued, disrespected, or disregarded. You then self-righteously crave to get revenge for this wrong-doing, immediately. It's like you believe that you can only bring the other person to justice by attacking them.

Regaining Emotional Equilibrium:

Since your thinking has been distorted or exaggerated by the anger, if you have any hope of regaining your emotional equilibrium, you must re-evaluate what happened from an adult point of view. This will need to happen before you can calm yourself. That's why the first thing you must do is calm yourself down, then you can move onto the second part of the process of getting your mind calm.

Find your Relaxation:

Hopefully, you already know how to calm yourself down when needed, whether it's deep breathing, meditation, music, guided imagery or visualization, yoga, acupressure, self-hypnosis, or another technique that works for you. However, if you haven't yet, you need to learn one first and foremost. Here are some ideas for doing that:

- **Research Breathing Exercises:** You could start by researching breathing exercises online, going with the one that seems most relevant to your situation. Stick with practicing this every day until you can pull it out and use it anytime you need to calm down.

- **Visualization:** For those who are more visually oriented, visualization can help a lot for relaxation. Imagine that you're on your favorite beach, taking a walk through a park, lying back on a floating cloud, next to a calm lake, or some other natural scene that feels relaxed to you. After you see the image in your mind, make sure you feel it in your body completely, reacting to these visual cues. Immersion is key here for effectiveness.

If you are picturing being at the beach, for example, fantasize about smelling the air, seeing the landscape, hearing the waves against the shore, and feeling the sun on your face. The more of your senses you engage at this stage, the more success you will have. Your body cannot sense the difference between a well-imagined scenario and a true experience.

Remember, however, that no matter what technique you use to calm yourself down and reduce your physical arousal levels, even if it's just deep breathing, will work for this. The most important consideration is that instead of ventilating your anger, you pause and soothe yourself. You will find that this reduces your anger significantly.

And in the case that you still cannot relax yourself using these techniques, instead, try some exercise. Vigorous physical activity can be a method for releasing the tension in your body from your angry mood. These actions will allow your body to calm down, along with your mind, so that you can again think in a clear manner and find a solution. That brings us to the second step in this process.

Step Number 2: Re-Consider.

The second step is to re-assess and re-consider your situation, meaning find a way to see the situation from a positive, different point of view. Anger comes primarily from a negative attitude about what occurred. Change this outlook and your feelings around it will also change. You can ask yourself some of the following questions to do this:

- Did they actually mean what I thought they meant? Perhaps I am making assumptions about something before verifying the facts.
- Is this event as bad as I am making it out to be, or could I be exaggerating the situation and taking it too hard?
- Is the belief I have that this person is unjust a reflection of my own bias, rather than proof that they are unfair? Are their concerns and interests equally important as mine are?
- Is there a way I can shift my focus to something more positive instead of just thinking about what I dislike about the situation?
- What evidence is there that this person wanted to humiliate, hurt, or antagonize me intentionally? Do I need to take this so personally?
- Is there a way to view this person's objectives with more empathy instead of making them into the enemy?

- Did this person have a rational reason to say what they did? Maybe I can learn from what they have said to me instead of getting so angry.
- Is there a chance that they misunderstood me? Perhaps I wasn't as clear as I could have been and that's why they had such a negative reaction to what happened.
- Was that person joking, by chance? Perhaps my insecurities are what is making me feel so upset and angry.
- If they are truly nasty, mean, and inconsiderate to me, is there a situation where I have also done this to someone else?

There are likely 100 or more questions you could ask yourself any time you are feeling angry and vulnerable. Hopefully, these examples are enough to get the point across. Your anger didn't come from what happened, but the interpretation, negative meaning, or perception that you placed upon it. So you must come up with different ways to view what it was that angered you. Nearly every time, you will notice that a more measured, level-headed assessment of the event that caused this angry reaction will help to dissolve it.

Methods for being Gentler and less Angry:

When you have less anger on a daily basis, you will feel happier and more relaxed. Keep in mind that what happens in your life is only external and that you are the one who chooses to respond that way to them internally. Remind yourself consistently that no one else can force you to be mad and that ultimately, this intense emotion was created in your head, nowhere else. Here are some methods for keeping your anger under control, instead of allowing it to blaze out of control and cause problems:

- **Smile:** Any time you get angry because of a stranger, try smiling at them instead. This will disarm the person, who won't expect that reaction, but intentionally pausing the anger in its tracks can give you some much-needed perspective.

- **Count to 10:** There's a reason why this is age old wisdom that we all know about. Next time you feel angry, stop and count to 10, breathing deeply so you can regain a rational sense of mind.

- **Understand the Source:** Are you the type that gets angry easily with hardly any instigation? Maybe someone caused you pain as a child and now easily fall into the belief that you are being victimized, even when you aren't. Understanding where this tendency to get angry fast came from can help you rise above the emotion when it strikes.

- **Don't Pay Attention to Aggression:** When you feel tempted to add to the spread of anger over the Internet, resist it. The first step is noticing when you want to feed the fire, then resisting that impulse.

- **Notice other Perspectives:** When a person annoys you because they are delivering bad news, don't automatically believe that they are intentionally causing you pain. Most customer service workers aren't trying to personally wrong you. Think about being in their shoes before you react in anger.

Perhaps by learning to control your own anger, you can make the world a better place and inspire calmer, happier actions in others.

Chapter 5: Long-lasting Anger

If you think that your anger problem is spiraling out of control, it's ruining your job or relationships, you may think about doing some counseling to find better ways to handle it. A licensed mental health practitioner can help you come up with methods for changing your actions and the thinking behind your anger.

Before choosing a counselor, you will likely meet with a few prospects. When you do, let them know that you have an anger problem that needs some work, or finds out about their anger management methods. There's nothing wrong with getting professional help, and for some anger issues, this may be the only way to truly heal.

Minimizing the Effects of Anger:

Sure, therapy isn't the only way to develop better methods for dealing with anger, but it can help you get in touch with your emotions and find better ways to show them. A lot of people who struggle with anger have this problem. Therapy can help you move to a more neutral anger range within two to three months, depending on the methods and circumstances.

Anger Management and Assertiveness Training:

Angry people must first learn assertiveness (as opposed to aggression), but the majority of courses and books about becoming more assertive are marketed for those who aren't in touch with their anger. The ones these books are written tend to be more on the passive side of things than is most common, allowing people to take advantage of them. This is not what someone who struggles with an anger problem does. But books such as these can still contain some useful information for controlling your frustration and being more assertive and constructive in conversation.

Remember, you can never completely get rid of anger, and even if you could, it wouldn't be smart or healthy. Regardless of how much you try to change the fact, events will always occur in life that leads you to feel angry, and at times, you will be justified in that anger.

Changing your Reactions and Attitudes:

Life will always come with loss, pain, frustration, and annoyance caused by what others do. You can never change this, but you can alter the way you react to these events and people. Getting your anger under control now will give you more lasting happiness in the future.

The Habit of Logic

If you can get into the habit of using logic when you get angry, you can defeat your anger. When anger occurs, even unjustified, it can easily spiral into the irrational. So if you use rational logic to defuse it, telling yourself that the world isn't against you, you're just having a hard day, it will become much easier. This can be done every time you feel your anger threatening to take over and beat you, and it will bring you a point of view that is much more balanced.

Becoming aware of your Demanding Ways:

People who get angry often usually demand what they want, whether it's willingness from others, agreement on their ideas, appreciation, or general fairness. All humans wish for these things and get disappointed and hurt when they don't work out. However, angry people demand these things and get disappointed, then mad when others don't meet their demands.

Prefer, don't Demand:

As a way to restructure your habits, you can begin becoming aware of this tendency in yourself and start using words such as "I would prefer" or "I'd like this" instead of demanding things to be a certain way. When you don't get what you wish for, you'll likely become disappointed, frustrated, and hurt, but anger won't be as common for you. A lot of angry people believe that if they jump to being mad, they are avoiding their pain, but the pain doesn't go away, it's just hidden under another layer and being expressed in another way.

Learning better Communication Habits:

People who get angry a lot often jump to conclusions, then act on them without thinking much into it. The problem is that their conclusions are often false, especially when jumped to in the heat of the moment. What you should do next time you are having a heated discussion is a pause, and give some thought to how you will respond.

- **Careful Consideration:** Saying the first thing you want to say when you get mad is a recipe for disaster. Instead, carefully consider what you want to communicate and the best way to do this.
- **Listen Carefully:** As you consider your responses, make sure you are also listening closely to the person

you're speaking with. Try to also listen to what lies beneath the anger. For example, maybe you want some space while your partner is seeking to be closer. If they begin complaining about how you're acting, resist the urge to tell them they are clingy or wrong for feeling the way they do.

- **Pay Attention to the Defensive Signal:** Defensiveness is a quick way to get into a fight with someone else, and it's only natural to feel defensive if you are getting criticized, but resist the urge to fight back. Rather, pay attention to what is underneath the words being spoken. Perhaps your partner is feeling unloved and neglected. You may need some time to calm down before discussing, but don't allow your anger to make the talk spiral into a bad place. Staying calm is the difference between a huge fight and a constructive discussion.

Restructuring your Brain:

To put this simply, it involves changing your thinking habits. People who are angry usually swear, curse, or speak in intense, negative terms that express their feelings and thoughts.

- **Replacing Dramatic Phrases:** When you're mad, your ways of thinking tend to be overly dramatic and ridiculously exaggerated. You can stall the storm by replacing these dramatic thoughts with more reasonable ideas. For example, rather than saying to yourself "This day is ruined, everything is awful," say "This is frustrating, and it's reasonable to get upset, but being angry won't solve anything."

- **Avoid Absolutes:** Part of dramatic, negative thinking relies on using absolute statements. Pay attention to your thoughts and words and make sure you don't use the words "always" or "never." Using statements like these only make you feel as though your madness is fair and justified and that no solution exists. In addition, this can humiliate and alienate those you are speaking to and prevent agreements.

Most importantly, get into the habit of reminding yourself that being angry won't fix the problem and will make you less likely to find a workable solution for the problem.

Switching up your Environment:

At times, it's your surroundings that are causing you to feel angry and irritated. Responsibilities and problems can pile up on you until you feel like you're about to explode. Remember to give yourself some time to decompress every once in a while. Just 20 minutes of quiet time to yourself can make all the difference between staying calm and acting out of anger.

Chapter 6: Being Angry at Yourself

When you're angry at yourself, simple tools of relaxation, such as relaxing visualization and deep breathing, can help to calm you. Many angry people would believe that this is too simple to actually work, but they are selling themselves short, in that case.

<u>Simple Relaxation Tools:</u>

Oftentimes, we give ourselves excuses like that just to avoid making the changes that need to be made in ourselves. There are courses and other books that give effective techniques for relaxation, and learning them gives you a new toolset to use in all situations.

If you are married to or dating someone who is also hot-tempered, both of you would benefit from learning techniques such as these. Here are some techniques you can begin practicing today.

Breathing Techniques:

The first technique involves breathing deeply, from your belly instead of your chest. Trying to breathe deeply from the chest is not relaxing. Instead, picture it coming from deep inside of your abdomen.

Using a Mantra:

Use a repeated mantra to keep yourself calm, such as "take it easy" or "relax." As you breathe deeply, say this to yourself again and again until it becomes automatic.

Stretching:

Stretching can be a good way to diffuse tension and anger in yourself, relaxing your body and helping you feel a lot calmer. Stretching feels great and instantly helps you feel better.

Sticking to it:

Perhaps the most important technique of all is remaining dedicated to learning how to relax when you get angry. After a while, you will be able to call upon these techniques any time you start to feel frustrated.

Effective Problem-Solving:

At times, our frustration and anger are caused by inescapable, real issues that we are dealing with. Not all of our anger is unjustified and is often a natural, healthy way of reacting to difficult situations. We also have an expectation that for every problem, a solution exists, so we get extra frustrated when this isn't true, sometimes. The best way to deal with situations such as this, then, is not to think about the solution, but to think about your attitude in regards to the problem at hand.

- **Come up with a Plan:** Create a plan and check in on your progress as you go. Decide that you are going to try your best but don't punish yourself when things don't go exactly as you would prefer the to go.

- **Keeping Patience:** Remember that if you can approach problems with the best of efforts and intentions and give it your all, you will have a lot easier of a time staying patient, even in the face of difficulties. This way, you will stay logical, even when the issue doesn't go away immediately.

Using Silly Humor to Defuse Anger:

Humor can help you get rid of anger in a few different ways. Primarily, it can give you a perspective that is more logical and balanced.

Picturing bad Names:

When you're mad and want to call someone a bad name, like a dirtbag, instead, pause and think about the word literally. For instance, you would picture a huge bag of dirt sitting in front of you. Doing this can help you calm down instantly, and humor is always helpful for tense situations.

Using your Imagination:

The main message that an angry person tells themselves is that they should always get their way, that they are to the right, and that they should never have to be inconvenienced, even if other people do. Next time you feel these emotions, picture yourself like a king or queen, walking the streets and stores, always getting your way while other people have to answer to you. If you can be very detailed in this imagining, you will likely realize that you're not very reasonable and that what you're worried about isn't that important.

Be Careful with Humor:

If you do use humor to defuse your anger, you should be cautious. Don't attempt to use it to laugh off or ignore your problems, but instead to see them in a more constructive way. Also, don't mistake healthy humor for angry sarcasm, which is just another way of expressing unhealthy anger patterns.

Other Techniques for Going Easier on Yourself:

These techniques all have one thing in common; remembering not to take life, or yourself, so seriously. Anger does feel serious, sure, but the ideas behind it can seem funny from the right perspective.

- **Changing Timing:** If your spouse and you have a pattern of arguing when you talk in the evening, maybe this is due to being distracted, tired, or just having a bad habit. You can shake this up by changing what time of day you talk.

- **Avoid Stress Triggers:** If you feel stressed out each time, you see your daughter's messy room, close her door instead of making it a habit of focusing on what makes you angry. The point is not to justify your anger and keep it there but to learn how to become calmer.

- **Look for Alternatives:** Pay attention to what triggers your anger, such as commuting through heavy traffic on the way home from work. Then you can learn to plan around this and find alternatives, such as finding a better route.

The quickest way to make your anger worse is to feel guilty about it or beat yourself up. Remember to forgive yourself for feeling angry.

Chapter 7: Healthy Outlets for your Anger

Anger is a healthy, normal feeling, but it can be unhealthy when it gets out of control or flares up very often. Explosive, chronic anger will lead to serious problems for your health, relationships, and mental state. Thankfully, you can get your anger under control, and it may be easier than you thought. As soon as you figure out why you feel so angry and use the tools given to you in this book, you can keep your anger from taking over your everyday life.

Why should you Control but not Smother Anger?

Anger is neither bad nor good. Similar to our other feelings, anger is giving us a message, letting us know that something threatening, unjust, or upsetting is occurring. If you feel anger and have the reaction of wanting to explode, though, you have no chance to heed this message. So although it's normal to feel anger when something goes wrong, you're wronged, or someone mistreats you, anger is an issue when you are harming other people or yourself by expressing it.

Anger Facts and Myths:

If your temper is hot, you might think that you can't control it, but it's possible to learn healthier ways to express your feelings. You're in control, not your emotion.

The Myth: You shouldn't hold your anger in, it's better to vent it.

The Fact:

Although it's true that ignoring your anger isn't good for you, letting it out without discrimination isn't any better. Anger doesn't need to be let free in a forceful or aggressive way to prevent yourself from exploding. Actually, tirades and outbursts just add to the problem, reinforcing it.

The Myth: Intimidation, aggression, and anger will get you what you want.

The Fact:

You can't get others to truly respect you through bullying them. They might be afraid, but you cannot handle differing opinions if you have no control over your anger. Other people are far more likely to listen and work with you if you are more respectful in your communication.

The Myth: Anger is out of your control and cannot be changed.

The Fact:

You cannot control every situation you come into contact with, or even the way you feel about it, but you have control over the way you express these feelings. Anger can be expressed without physical or verbal abuse. Even when another person is really getting on your nerves, your response is always a choice.

Being Honest about your Anger:

You may believe that showing your anger every time it comes up is healthy, that other people are too thin-skinned, that you have every justification for being mad, or that you must show anger for others to take you seriously. But the fact of the matter is that this emotion will impair your better judgment, hurt those around you, and have an overall bad effect on your self-image and how others view you.

- **The Point of Managing Your Anger:** A lot of people believe that anger management relies on avoiding or suppressing angry feelings, but the goal is not to never feel mad. Anger is healthy and normal, as stated before, and will be expressed even if you try to avoid it. Your goal with learning how to manage is not to avoid or suppress it but to have a deeper understanding of what the feeling is trying to tell you, and find better ways to express it. This will help you feel better, meet your needs, manage confrontation and conflict, and have stronger, healthier relationships.

- **The Importance of Practice:** Managing anger is not the easiest thing you will ever do, but practice will make it much easier and the benefits are endless. When you learn how to both control and healthily express this feeling, you will be a lot likelier to reach the success you dream of.

The Dangers of Rampant Anger:

Anger that runs out of control is harmful to your physical body. Living with high-stress levels will leave you open to a higher chance of insomnia, a weak immune system, diabetes, heart and blood pressure issues. What else can it do?

- **Harm you Mentally:** Long-lasting anger will take up large amounts of your thought space and mental energy, clouding your reasoning abilities and making it much more difficult to enjoy life or even concentrate on anything. It will cause you depression, anxiety, and over harmful mental issues if not looked at.

- **Harm you Professionally:** Creative differences, constructive critique, and even heated arguments can lead to healthy results. However, lashing out in frustration will only alienate you from your clients, supervisors, and co-workers, making them think less of you and have a harder time being honest.

- **Harm your Relationships:** Anger causes scars that don't disappear in the people you love. When you explode in anger, other people will be far less likely to trust you, be honest with you, or even want to be around you.

Look Beneath the Emotion:

To reach healthy outlets for your anger, you must first look beneath the emotion itself. Anger issues usually come from things you learned in childhood. If you saw your parents yell, throw things, and argue all the time, you may believe that these are normal expressions of frustration or anger. High-stress levels and trauma as a kid can also leave you open to bad anger habits, as well.

- **Anger hides Other Emotions:** To learn how to express anger in healthy and appropriate ways, first, you have to get in touch with your true feelings. Are your outbursts there to mask other emotions like vulnerability, shame, hurt, insecurity, or embarrassment? If you have a common response to anger, you are probably using it to hide other emotions.

- **Looking to your Upbringing:** If you grew up in a situation where sharing emotion wasn't encouraged, this is even more likely. Now that you've grown up, you might have difficulty noticing any emotions apart from frustration or anger. In addition, anger can signal other health issues like chronic stress or trauma.

Is there more to this Emotion in you?

It can be hard to tell if your anger is just anger or if there's more beneath this emotion in you. Here are some signs that your anger is harboring more than it appears to be:

- **You can't Compromise:** Do you have difficulty understanding the perspectives of others or conceding your points of view? If you had an upbringing surrounded by out of control anger, you might be imitating patterns that you observed as a kid, believing that anger will get you what you want. The idea of compromise might make you feel vulnerable or like a failure.

- **You aren't in Touch with other Emotions:** Are you a tough person who is always in control of situations, no matter what? Do you think that feelings such as shame, guilt, or fear are not part of your life? Every person has those feelings, so if you think you don't, you're likely using aggression or anger to cover them up.

- **Opinions that are Different from yours are a Challenge:** If you think that you're always right and find yourself getting mad when people disagree, you could be using anger to mask your other emotions. If you see differing opinions as a challenge instead of a varied perspective, you probably need to look closer at your anger.

Reconnecting with Feelings:

If you find yourself getting uncomfortable at the thought of emotions other than anger, or getting stuck in a familiar, harmful response to disruptions in your life, you need to learn how to reconnect with your emotions. The first step is to start noticing your anger triggers and warning signs.

- **The Physical Signs:** Although you probably think that your anger appears out of nowhere with no warning, there are warning signals that show up on a physical level when anger starts. Anger is just one of the many physical responses humans can feel and fuels the fight or flight function in us. The madder you get, the stronger this reaction will be. When you start to notice these signs, you can manage the flow of anger before it takes over.
- **Physical Examples:** Physical signs of anger present in your body include a knotted stomach, clenching your jaw or hands, feeling flushed or clammy, faster breathing, headaches, needing to move or pace, and having difficulty concentrating. You might also tense up your shoulders or have a pounding heart.

Thought Patterns that cause Anger:

You might believe that situations outside of you, such as other people's actions, are what lead to your anger. However, anger issues have more to do with your thoughts about a situation than the actual situation. Here are some negative patterns of thought that can cause you to feel very angry:

- **Overgeneralization**: Overgeneralizing can lead you to feel very angry. For example, saying "Everyone is so disrespectful to me" is a quick way to get mad.

- **Assuming:** Trying to read people's minds or making assumptions can cause you to feel disrespected and thus angry.
- **Having "should" Thoughts:** When you have a rigid idea of how things must go, you will get mad when circumstances don't align with that idea.
- **Blaming Others:** When something doesn't go right, an angry person will always look for someone else to blame. Instead of taking responsibility, you will blame someone else for what has happened to you.
- **Looking for Reasons to be Upset:** Angry people often search for reasons to be upset, blowing things out of proportion or ignoring the positive. Allowing these irritations to build up can cause you to explode over something small.

Who Stresses You Out?

If you struggle with anger, you probably have a few circumstances or people in your life that lead to this emotion. If there is a person who consistently angers you, this could be a signal that you shouldn't spend as much time around them. There will always be people you have to be around with no choice in the matter, such as an irritating boss or co-worker, but in terms of the people you choose to be around, it might be wise to take an inventory of who is causing you stress and spend less time around them.

Remembering to Calm yourself:

As soon as you can recognize the signs that your anger is on the rise, you can handle it fast before it hurts you or those around you. You can start by focusing on how the anger makes you feel physically. Although it sounds counterintuitive, paying attention to these signals can actually lessen the intensity of the frustration at the moment.

Massage yourself:

You can calm yourself down by reaching back to massage your neck and shoulders. Don't forget to breathe deeply, in addition to this, especially by going outside to get some fresh air. Try to get all of your senses engaged with your surroundings, picturing your favorite place, listening to your favorite music, and immersing yourself in your environment.

Reality Checks:

When your anger is threatening to take over, you can bring yourself back to a calmer state by doing reality checks. As soon as you begin to get upset, pause and consider what's happening, asking yourself some of the following questions:

- How much does this matter in the big picture?

- Is this worth feeling horrible over?

- Should I really ruin my day with this?

- Is my reaction reasonable or appropriate?

- How can I change this situation?

- Is it worthwhile to take action and change this?

Once you have decided that what's happening is actually worth your anger, and you can do something to change it, the next step is expressing the anger in a constructive and healthy manner. When you communicate and channel your anger effectively and respectfully, it can be a great inspiration and energy source for changing your life or the issue at hand.

Get Specific about the Feeling:

Another useful way to defuse your anger and work with it in a healthy way is to pinpoint the true feeling behind your anger. Have you been in a fight over something trivial and ridiculous? Huge fights can happen over nothing, such as forgetting to take the trash out, but there is typically something larger happening beneath this.

Walk Away if Needed:

When you find your anger spiraling out of control, take yourself out of the situation so you can cool down. A quick burst of exercise, a walk around the block, meditation, or listening to a song can give you time to cool off, release the emotion, and come back to the problem with a more solution-oriented mindset.

Be Fair in your Fights:

It's fine to get mad at someone. However, without fair fighting, you will see that the relationship breaks down quite fast. Fair fights will let you share what you need while listening to and respecting the other. This is the only way to reach a positive resolution when it comes to interpersonal issues.

Other Healthy Ways to Let Anger out:

If you notice your anger and irritation is on the rise, ask yourself what you're truly getting angry over. Finding out what is causing your frustration will aid you in communicating the feeling in a constructive way and finding a good resolution. You can also follow some of these tips to get your anger under control:

- **Be Present:** As soon as you are caught up in anger's heat, it can be easy to throw out insults or other expressions of frustration, either for yourself or other people. It's also easy to blame others for the way you are or the difficult aspects of your life. Instead of blaming others from the past, think about the present moment from a mindset of finding solutions.

- **Prioritize the Relationship:** Next time you find yourself getting mad in an interpersonal situation, make strengthening and maintaining the relationship more important than being the winner of the argument. This will help you respect the other person. Confrontations and conflicts are tiring, so start thinking about whether your anger is worth this energy. When you fight and argue over every tiny issue, other people are not going to take your concerns seriously.

- **Forgiveness:** Fixing conflicts (either with others or yourself) is impossible without forgiveness. Finding solutions relies on getting rid of the desire to punish other people, which doesn't help. To truly get past your anger problem, you have to learn how to let things go when needed. If you aren't able to agree on something, agree to move past it. When a conflict is just getting worse, sometimes it's best to walk away.

- **Conflict Resolution:** Your pattern for responding to disagreements and differences at work and home can lead to riffs and hostility, or it can lead to trust and safety, depending on how you handle things. Strengthening your conflict resolution skills will lead to better relationships and a lessened anger problem for you.

Finding Professional Help for your Anger:

If you still find that, even after trying all of the tools in this book, your anger is taking over, you may need some more help. Many programs, classes, and therapists exist to help people with anger issues. This can be helpful because you'll connect with others who understand your plight.

- **Practicing new Skills:** Therapy for anger management can help you find out why you feel so angry. Many people have anger but don't know where it's coming from, which makes it nearly impossible to control. Therapy can help you identify your anger triggers in a healthy, safe environment. It will also teach you new skills for expressing it.
- **Groups or Classes:** Groups or classes for anger management let you hear the accounts of other people who are going through the same struggle. This will teach you techniques and tips for managing frustration.

When to Consider Professional Assistance:

If the following apply to you, it's time to think about professional assistance for managing your anger:

- You are always angry or frustrated, even after trying to calm yourself down.

- Your anger leads to a relationship or work problems consistently.

- You've been in legal trouble because of your frustration and anger.

- Your frustration has caused physical altercations.

- If a family member has issues with anger that affect you.

Dealing with a Family Member's Anger:

If it's your relative or other loved one that has an issue with anger, you are probably always afraid of setting them off. But keep in mind that it's not your fault that they are angry. Verbally or physically abusive behavior is never okay. You should be able to expect respect, but when you are being disrespected, you can control the way you handle it and respond. Here are some tips for handling this in a positive way.

- Set personal boundaries so that they know what you are not prepared to tolerate.
- Discuss the problem when you are not fighting instead of when you're both already angry.
- Don't hesitate to remove yourself and walk away if your relative or loved one refuses to get calm.

- Think about therapy or counseling if you can't assert yourself when this person lashes out at you.
- Make sure you are taking your own safety seriously and remove yourself if your safety feels threatened.

The real issue with abusive relationships is not anger. Abuse and domestic violence are actually methods people use to control others, not just an issue of the loss of control. If you're part of a relationship that is abusive, couple's therapy is not the answer. Your partner may need special treatment and counseling, not just classes or group therapy.

Conclusion

Thank you for reading *Anger Management: 7 Steps to Freedom from Anger, Stress, and Anxiety.* Hopefully, this book has given you a better understanding of the origins of anger, justified versus unjustified anger, the benefits of this feeling, and the dangers it can present.

If you don't learn to handle your anger in constructive ways now, you will risk serious health problems, difficulties forming and keeping relationships, and trouble in every other area of life. Give yourself the gift of freedom from this emotion and start living the life you were meant to live!

Keep in mind that the more you practice these tactics and methods, the easier it will be to control your anger problem and choose healthier responses to this feeling inside of you. Eventually, you will notice that your anger has less control over your life.

Thank you for reading and good luck on your path to emotional wellness.

Thank you!

Before you go, I just wanted to say thank you for purchasing my book.

You could have picked from dozens of other books on the same topic but you took a chance and chose this one.

So, a HUGE thanks to you for getting this book and for reading all the way to the end.

Now I wanted to ask you for a small favor. **Could you please take just a few minutes to leave a review for this book on Amazon?**

This feedback will help me continue to write the type of books that will help you get the results you want. So if you enjoyed it, please let me know! (-:

Made in the USA
San Bernardino, CA
12 May 2018